TRUE CRIMES FROM THE PAST

C000175648

Kent

W.H.Johnson

COUNTRYSIDE BOOKS
NEWBURY BERKSHIRE

First published 2005
© W.H. Johnson, 2005

All rights reserved. No reproduction
permitted without the prior permission
of the publisher:

COUNTRYSIDE BOOKS
3 Catherine Road
Newbury, Berkshire

To view our complete range of books,
please visit us at
www.countrysidebooks.co.uk

ISBN 1 85306 939 6
EAN 978 1 85306 939 0

Designed by Peter Davies, Nautilus Design
Produced through MRM Associates Ltd., Reading
Typeset by Jean Cussons Typesetting, Diss, Norfolk
Printed by Woolnough Bookbinding Ltd., Irthlingborough

CONTENTS

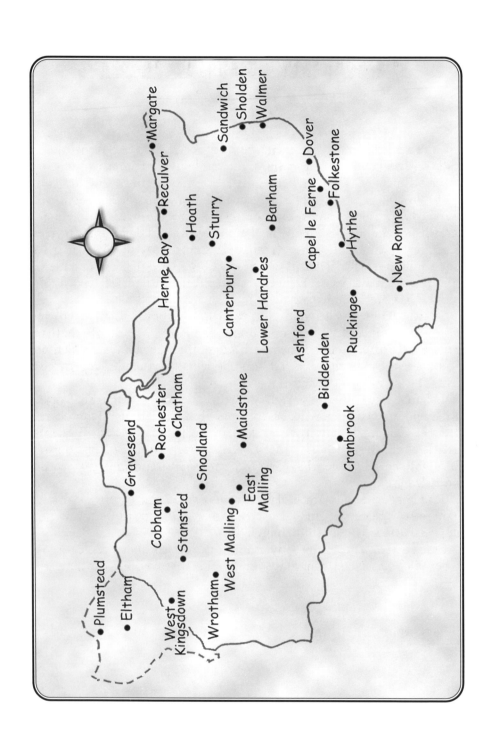

ACKNOWLEDGEMENTS

In writing this collection of Kent murder cases, I have been very dependent on many other people. As always the Kent library service has come up trumps, responding as promptly as staffing demands permit. They have been truly impressive and I should like to place on record my thanks to individual libraries at Ashford, Broadstairs, Deal, Folkestone, Maidstone and Margate. I am equally grateful to the libraries at Gillingham (Medway), Lewisham, Bromley, Eastbourne and to Greenwich Heritage Centre. My thanks also go to the Landesmuseum, Zurich, who responded so promptly to my queries about the British Swiss Legion. As ever Paul Williams' Murder Files service has been invaluable.

Martin Webb of Egerton wrote an instant response to my email and clarified an important matter. I hope that Barry Meade of Chatham Historical Society will not be too disappointed that I have decided not to pursue the case that I asked him about but his detailed reply to me cannot go without recognition.

I should like to thank various contributors to the magazine Bygone Kent and in particular W.H. Bishop, Julie Deller, George Frampton and Harold Gough. It would be remiss not to mention Gerry Edwards' article about the death of PC May in the Police History Society Journal. It is not the first time that Gerry has filled in important gaps in my knowledge.

And I am especially grateful to Michael and Martin George who have generously permitted me to use one of the illustrations from their impressive book, *Coast of Conflict*.

Finally, thanks to Anne, my wife, both for her sharp critical sense when it comes to spotting flaws in the narrative and for her patience.

INTRODUCTION

I hope that this book of murders, based on the old county of Kent, will be as warmly received as have my previous books. This time I have included more cases from the 19th and early 20th centuries particularly because I wanted the chance to bring in some relative newcomers, murders which have had very little exposure. For instance, I have known about the Bodle murder for a long time but have not seen it written up anywhere. As I believe that it has all the qualities of a genuine classic, here is an account of that most intriguing case in the chapter entitled 'The Eleven Year Murder Mystery'. Another case that I have long wanted to write is also included: it is 'The Wicked Stepmother', the story of the last woman to be publicly hanged in England. The same kind of scenario is played out these days too. There are warning signs of children in danger from the adults nearest to them, and all too frequently nothing is done until it is too late and some or other adult mutters something about 'lessons being learnt'. Alas, these lessons are too rarely learnt.

I have also wanted to write about the case of the Serb mercenary soldier, Dedea Redanies, who murdered the Back sisters. This crime, with all its horror, still puzzles me – a crime committed by a young man who on the face of things was essentially decent. What drove him to such an act?

There are only two or three relatively well-known cases in this book. The Stratton brothers' dark murder, involving two thugs and their old, helpless victims, is of a kind that is endlessly repeated. If their trial did not mark a significant development in forensic history they would be forgotten. The other murder with which readers may have some acquaintance is that of 16-year-old Nellie Trew on Eltham Common. This included some truly excellent detective work. And the murder of Caroline Trayler is still perhaps recalled by some. It is interesting largely because of the way that, due to a technical hitch in the legal procedures, the killer walked free.

But enough, it's time to start reading the cases.

W.H. Johnson

THE ELEVEN YEAR MURDER MYSTERY

eorge Bodle's farm, Montague House, is extensive, with fine barns and granaries. Years earlier, during the Napoleonic Wars, like many farmers, he made a considerable amount of money. The 81-year-old farmer, a churchwarden, is well known and highly respected in the district. His substantial house, situated in the High Street, is surrounded by well-tended hedges. At the side of the house runs a cart track, overhung with apple trees, heavy with blossom in spring and, in summer, laden with fruit. By the roadside there is a

Contemporary sketch of Montague House, John Bodle's farm at Plumstead.

7

kitchen garden where these days the old man potters. A stream runs to a pond at the rear of the house. Here is the orchard, at the end of which a gate leads to a cottage where Bodle's son John, known locally as a womaniser, lives with his wife and two sons, George and Young John.

It is idyllic here. It is Plumstead. It is 1833. And George Bodle is, in today's terms, a millionaire.

But it is no longer summer now. Autumn trails its way out and it is dark this second day of November. Even so, at six o'clock in the morning there is a bustle about the place. Several of the servants sleep in the house and already they are at work by candlelight. Henry Parker, the cowboy (so he is described), is off to bring in the cattle for milking. Sophia Taylor, a Foots Cray girl, has already lit the fire and is now cleaning the stove. Shortly she will have to set about making the breakfasts. Then there will be the churning to do and the preparing of the meals for the rest of the day. Of course, Elizabeth Smith, the deaf and dumb girl, is there to help her with the day's chores and so is old Mrs Lear who does some of the cleaning. And, fortunately, Mrs Elizabeth Evans, Mrs Bodle's daughter from her first marriage, has been staying for the past three days and she can be quite helpful. But it is hard toil for all of them.

Young John breezes in this Saturday morning and, seeing Sophia on her knees at the stove, asks if there's anything he can do to help. 'Nothing that I know of,' she tells him but there's so much to do and it's good-natured of him to ask, she thinks. It always gets the day off to a good start when Young John arrives with his cans to collect the milk for his family. For the past fortnight he has come down every morning early and sat around and talked and sometimes has made himself useful in small ways. He's such fun and he tells jokes and there was the time he even dressed up in woman's clothes and made them all laugh. Sophia really enjoys it when he comes and so does Elizabeth Smith. And they have a kind of flirtatious relationship, Sophia and Young John, and she has played the odd joke on him. It helps the morning along. After all she is only 20 and he is just 22.

Sophia goes down to the cellar for the milk while he opens the window shutters in the kitchen and washhouse for her. And then he goes out to the pump in the yard, just outside the kitchen door, and fills the great iron kettle. It's usually Henry Parker's task but he's with the cattle this morning, and Young John has offered to do it. And when Sophia comes back, there's the kettle already hanging over the fire.

Shortly after this Young John leaves with his cans of milk. When the kettle boils Sophia fills the coffee pot and serves Mr Bodle's breakfast downstairs. Elizabeth Evans takes coffee and toast upstairs to her mother, who is unwell. The old people's immediate needs attended to, Mrs Evans, Elizabeth Smith and Sophia have their breakfasts together. They use the same coffee pot, just adding more boiling water.

Half an hour after breakfast Sophia meets Mr Bodle in the yard. He's been feeding the hens. She has just been very sick she tells him. She feels dreadful. So does he, he replies. He, too, has been sick. She's had two cups of coffee and wonders if that might be the cause.

In the course of the day the whole household is laid low. Elizabeth Smith is violently ill, as is Elizabeth Evans. Like the rest, old Mrs Bodle, already under the weather, is constantly vomiting, suffering severe attacks of diarrhoea. Only Henry Parker seems to have escaped. Perhaps he did not have breakfast with the rest. He is called on the rest of the day to help out with quite unfamiliar duties. Fortunately, Mrs Lear, the charwoman, is also unaffected. She has been lucky because, as usual, she was given the coffee grounds to take home, but when her daughter looked at what her mother had brought she thought they seemed unusually thick and didn't use them.

Stomach upsets are not unusual in this pre-Victorian world. People suffer but they usually recover. But by late afternoon the family and their servants are becoming concerned for themselves, all of them labouring under the same wretched symptoms. They wonder if they have caught cholera.

Dr Butler is summoned from Woolwich. On arrival at Montague House, he finds George Bodle in a serious condition. The old man has been violently sick eight or nine times and has acute stomach pains. He is intensely thirsty and has a burning sensation in the throat. The doctor asks all of them what they have had for breakfast and the common factor seems to be the coffee or the water. Mrs Lear has brought back the coffee grounds and the doctor takes them with him when he leaves. He goes to Woolwich, handing over the grounds to Mr Marsh, a 'practical chemist' at the Royal Arsenal. Perhaps the kettle, too, would have provided further information had not Parker been instructed by old Mr Bodle to scrape it out thoroughly with a chisel in case it had been the cause of the illness.

Over the next few days the patients recover at varying rates, although Sophia Taylor will be confined to bed for much of the following week.

And George Bodle will never recover. Still suffering greatly, and fearing that the water may be contaminated, he calls for a pint of ale. According to the doctor, it is this in part which prevents his recovery. He dies on the Tuesday. His body is examined by the doctor and two of his colleagues. The stomach is inflamed but it is the condition of the other organs that tells them definitely that the old man has died of arsenic poisoning. Mr Marsh confirms the presence of arsenic in the coffee pot though whether it was the water or the coffee itself will never be cleared up.

Is this a deliberate poisoning? And if so, are there suspicions and on whom do they fall? Of all people, Young John Bodle seems the likely candidate because, and it seems almost out of the blue, he has left Plumstead at a time when his grandfather is dying, when his grandmother is still sick, when the girls he has chaffed and joked with in recent days are ill. Is that not odd?

On the Wednesday the magistrates are given some confidential information that seems further to point him out as the poisoner. It is Young John's own father who carries this information to the magistrates. My son, he says, is guilty. And he mentions his wife, Young John's mother, as party to an incriminating conversation. John Bodle brings with him before the magistrates his servant, Mary Higgins, who overheard only a week ago some strange words.

According to Mary Higgins, Mrs John Bodle had said, 'John, I wish your father was dead.'

And Young John had answered, 'I wish that grandfather was dead.'

His grandfather?

'Because we should then have hundreds or thousands a year,' he had said.

And then he had gone on to say that he'd like his father to die one week and his grandfather the next.

Is this believable? Are such thoughts expressed so openly in front of the servants? For that matter, are they expressed so openly in front of anyone? Perhaps if the conversation did take place it was all in jest. At the time Mary Higgins had not taken the conversation seriously. But now, given the circumstances ... and given the information from the analyst, Mr Marsh, that there is arsenic in the coffee grounds ... and given the further information that Young John has twice in recent weeks purchased arsenic locally, there is need to send for him wherever he may be. He must be arrested at once. Arsenic, indeed. That's the poison the French call 'inheritance powder'.

Constable Morris, with a warrant for his arrest, is told where his quarry is. Young John has gone off to Clerkenwell, to his sister's house, and it is there that he is arrested on the Wednesday. 'You cannot want me,' he protests. 'It must be my brother George you want.' At this point he faints and Morris handcuffs him and the pair travel back to Plumstead by horse-drawn public omnibus. At Plumstead he is confined in the Cage, the local lock-up. And now he tells the constable that he will find two packages and a bottle in his trunk at home. Morris collects what is surely valuable evidence although he has a misfortune with the bottle, which he drops. He explains that the accident happened while he was bending down to fasten his shoelaces but his superiors believe him to have taken too much alcohol in the course of his busy day and he is placed under suspension. Nevertheless, the two packets are intact and they do contain arsenic. Can Young John Bodle really have poisoned his grandfather?

The inquest was held on the Thursday at the Plume of Feathers tavern in Plumstead before the coroner, Mr J. Carttar. All of those concerned gave evidence: Dr Butler, Sophia Taylor (from her bed for she was unfit to attend); Elizabeth Evans; Henry Parker, the cowboy; Elizabeth Smith, the deaf and dumb girl, speaking through an interpreter; Mary Higgins whose master had told her to tell all she knew; Mr Marsh, the 'practical chemist'; and others who witnessed Young John's purchase of arsenic. Why should he have bought arsenic? Why was there such a quantity of the poison found in his trunk? Was that not a clear enough indication of his intentions?

The Plumstead lock-up, known as 'The Cage'.
(Courtesy of Greenwich Heritage Centre)

11

And motive? It was stated that George Bodle had made his will only a fortnight earlier although the disposition of his property was not stated. Perhaps the young man was trying to advance matters. Then it transpired that before the old man died 'he took an affectionate leave of his son but forbade Young John to enter the house.' Had George Bodle some inkling that his grandson had poisoned him?

Even so, there were those who spoke warmly of Young John. Sophia Taylor could not entertain the idea that Young John had attempted to poison her. She had known him since she came to work for Mr and Mrs Bodle two and half years earlier and had always been on good terms with him. 'He is a nice young man and I have nothing to say against him,' she insisted.

Elizabeth Smith now seemed to think that it was Henry Parker who put the kettle on – so frail are our memories for such ordinary daily details – and agreed that Young John was a very good-natured lad, always ready to lend a hand. As for Henry Parker, he was sure that the kettle was already filled when he came in but could not say who put it on the fire.

The Plume of Feathers, Plumstead. (Courtesy of Greenwich Heritage Centre)

Eventually, the coroner's jury reached a verdict of wilful murder, and Young John Bodle was committed to trial.

By the time the Maidstone Assizes opened on 12th December 1833 there was a swell of local sympathy in favour of the prisoner. Many in the jam-packed courtroom sympathised with the accused, sitting in the dock, dressed 'very genteelly in deep mourning'. In spite of all that had been said there were still many doubts surrounding the case. If anyone in that family could contemplate murder, surely it was not Young John. But his father, that notorious philanderer, mightn't he have need of money? Now there was a rascal. And so the rumours circulated.

There was the usual army of witnesses, repeating more or less what they had already recited at the inquest. Elizabeth Smith's sign reader explained that the girl was certain that Young John Bodle put the kettle on. For his part, however, Henry Parker was unable to remember saying at the inquest that he found the kettle filled and that someone else put it on the fire. He was now certain that he himself put the kettle on. At least he was until he again became uncertain about the matter.

Dr Butler was lucid enough in the witness box but he was unable to clarify whether the poison had been put into the kettle or mixed with the coffee grounds. This was important for there was no suggestion that Young John had been near the coffee jar, which was kept locked away in a cupboard.

The apothecary, Joseph Evans, clearly recalled selling arsenic on two occasions to Young John. But he had not questioned the purchase. Plenty of people bought arsenic from him. If people did not keep a cat or if they did not care to set traps for rats they laid down arsenic. There was nothing out of the ordinary in buying arsenic and, until the present matter, Evans had not given any thought to the fact that Young John Bodle had purchased arsenic from him.

Sophia Taylor went through the oft-repeated tale of what happened in the kitchen on the morning of the poisoning. Then she was asked a question she could not answer. She had never heard that John Bodle, father of the accused, had recently been forbidden entry to his father's house. And no, she said in answer to further little probing queries, she had never known a woman called Hodges. Nor anyone called Mrs Shears nor yet another named Warwickshire. Nor had she ever heard of a Mrs Warren.

As for Elizabeth Evans, she too had never heard of John Bodle being banned from his father's house. This is an interesting point, which was not resolved at the trial. It is unclear still if and why and for what period John Bodle was denied access to the house. Certainly he was there at his father's bedside when he died and there is evidence that he went to the house to deal with farm matters. Perhaps George Bodle simply refused to meet his dissolute son socially.

More intriguing stuff came from Mrs Lear, some of which may clarify the old man's displeasure with his son. Though it seems on the face of it to have little to do with the death of George Bodle or with his accused grandson, there may be some pointers to a kind of secret history. Mrs Lear was asked if she knew a woman called Hodges living in Plumstead. Yes, she did, but no, she did not know that John Bodle 'has been living with that woman and that he has a family by her.' While she also knew 'a woman named Stevenson, Shoulder of Mutton Green', she did not know that 'she had a family by John Bodle'. Like Sophia Taylor, she expressed ignorance of any women called Warwickshire or Warren.

How long had she known Mr Bodle, Mrs Lear was asked. Several years, she said. And then, the next question is asked but the judge hurriedly intervenes and we never find out the answer to 'Did you not know him in Maidstone jail?' Secret history indeed.

Then comes Mary Higgins who had gone with her master, John Bodle, to the magistrates the day after George Bodle's death. She gives some unexceptional information about what occurred in John Bodle's kitchen on the morning of the poisoning. The routines were identical to those in the farmhouse only fifty yards or so away. She had got up before six o'clock and just like Sophia and Elizabeth had busied herself lighting the fire, taking down the shutters and so on. She remembered Young John was up especially and unusually early that morning and recalled his going to the farmhouse with the milk cans.

But it was the conversations that she had overheard that intrigued the court. She repeated the account that she had earlier given to the coroner's court and the magistrates. She told how she had heard Mrs Bodle and Young John talking together in the kitchen and how Mrs Bodle had said that she wished her husband were dead. That had apparently not caused Young John any surprise and he had gone on to say that he wished his grandfather were dead. The talk was all about money.

Even more dramatically, she spoke about Young John and his mother talking in the kitchen at about three o'clock on the Saturday afternoon. Old Mr Bodle and his wife, Mrs Evans and the servants were now all laid low. Young John had said to his mother that he would not mind poisoning anyone that he did not like. That was silly talk, his mother told him. And he had replied, 'Only give me the stuff and you'll see.' His mother answered that she wouldn't risk her own soul into danger for anyone.

On the second day of the trial the ladies' man, John Bodle, was in the witness box and, although he disagreed with some of Mary Higgins's testimony, he remembered her telling him that she had heard Young John remark that 'he had done for one party and would do for another and that he was satisfied with what he had done.'

Under cross-examination Bodle said, 'I believe I am entitled to have the bulk of my father's property after the death of my mother. I have never heard that he caused his will to be altered shortly before his death.'

And so, the defence implied, did he not have expectations? Did he not expect to benefit from his father's death?

But then John was rattled by the more probing questions about his personal life. 'I object to answer whether I have ever been charged with felony; or that I have ever been in Maidstone jail; or that I have families living by three different women besides my wife, or that I was ever charged with attempting to cut my wife's throat.'

This line of enquiry was stopped when the judge intervened but damage was being done all the time to the prosecution case. By the time he left the witness box there were some who wondered whether John Bodle was more likely to be the guilty party.

Then came the opportunity to hear Young John's side of things.

At that time counsel was not permitted to address the jury on behalf of clients. In his defence Young John handed in a long handwritten statement, which was read aloud by the clerk of the court. This document had been composed under the prisoner's instructions by his counsel, the solicitor Mr Colquhoun. It was a skilful declaration and made a strong impression. Most powerful is the way in which he deals with his father who had gone to the magistrates with false information. 'My father is the first person to accuse me of this crime. It is he who produces Mary Higgins as a witness to procure my condemnation. What can be the motive which has induced a father thus to conduct himself towards his child? Gentlemen, I grieve to say my father has not set a fit and worthy example before his family. It has been the lot of his children to see him imprisoned for malicious injury, and guilty of profligacy of all kinds, but still, the voice of nature cannot be dead within him. What is his overwhelming motive? Can any adequate reason be suggested except the desire to avert from himself the terrible consequences of this horrible offence? What a light does not this throw upon the whole mystery! My father had the run of the house and could do what he pleased with the coffee jar. In his anxiety to throw suspicion from himself, he eagerly accuses his own child, misrepresenting facts, swearing to a fabricated conversation with his servant, and exhibiting a line of conduct wicked, unnatural, and irreconcilable except by the dreadful explanation I suggest.'

John Bodle might have been denied access to his father but he had 'the run of the house'; he could roam the farmhouse, perhaps before anyone else rose. It gave him ample opportunity to poison the coffee.

As for Young John's absconding from home, there was no mystery about that. He had been invited to Clerkenwell by his sister and he had gone on the Tuesday, believing that the worst effects of the poison were over and unaware that his grandfather was on the point of dying.

And the arsenic he had bought? What about that? He explained that some years earlier he had the misfortune to be subject to an attack of 'the itch', brought home to the family by his father who had been cohabiting with a Mrs Warren. As a cure he used a mixture of arsenic and hellebore, a well-known remedy for what seems to have been syphilis. He had tried to keep quiet about it. But there was a witness to his ailment, Mrs Perks, a former landlady, who would testify that while he lived in her house at Shoreditch he had always kept arsenic in his trunk. To alleviate his condition, he used to mix arsenic with lard.

Reverting to the evidence of his father and Mary Higgins, Young John says, 'I feel I should be insulting your judgement if I thought you could believe one syllable of their story. You will recollect that my own father is the first person to accuse me of this dreadful crime. He it is who goes to the magistrate and puts this charge in motion against me. He it is who, after an interview with Mary Higgins, produces her as a witness to ensure my condemnation, by swearing to a conversation that never occurred, and in the relation of which they falter and equivocate in a manner you have heard.'

What, he asks, could induce someone to become 'not only the willing accuser of his child but the fabricator of false evidence against him'?

It was a highly effective defence.

Finally the judge began to sum up but he was interrupted by the jury foreman. The jury apparently had already resolved to find the prisoner not guilty. There was no need for his Lordship to outline the pros and cons.

And so, to immense excitement, to loud applause and cheers, to some tears of relief, Young John Bodle left the court. As he went, handkerchiefs waved joyfully from the gallery. Outside, he was received with open arms by his grandmother. All of the jurymen shook him by the hand. Back in Plumstead the whole village turned out to welcome him home. The following Sunday when he attended church, special thanks during prayers were offered for his delivery.

The case was never followed up. No charges were laid against John Bodle or Mary Higgins though for long years people had their own ideas of what had happened. It was all too obvious. Or it seemed to be.

Then, eleven years later, in February 1844, only four months after the death of the philandering John Bodle, there was a newspaper item that seems to resolve the mystery:

'During the past week much interest has been manifested in the localities of Plumstead, Charlton and Woolwich, in consequence of a report that [Young] John Bodle, who was tried and acquitted 11 years ago for the murder of his grandfather, had confessed to being the individual who perpetrated the atrocious deed which, from inquiries that have been instituted, turns out to be too well founded.

'On Tuesday afternoon last, John Bodle, who assumed the name of John Bardon Smith, was convicted at the Central Criminal Court before Mr Justice Coleridge, for extorting money by means of threats of a most abominable description from Mr Robinson, the butler of Lord Abingdon, some particulars of which appeared in our Marlborough Street police reports a few weeks since. There were two indictments laid against him; the court, however, only went into one, of which he was found guilty; but it is only right to say that if the second had been investigated it would have further shown the systematic course of villainy which he has for a length of time carried on; and the learned judge in passing a sentence of 20 years' transportation upon him, strongly commented upon the diabolical manner in which he had chosen to stigmatise his innocent victim. He had admitted his guilt in a letter which he had written in Newgate to Mr Robinson, the prosecutor, praying that he would forego the prosecution, as his conviction would cause the death of an only sister and prevent his union with a respectable lady of some property; and in conclusion that the charge he made against him he had completely trumped up in the hope of extorting some money.

'Since the prisoner's incarceration in Newgate, it has been communicated to the friends of the unfortunate deceased gentleman, Mr John Bodle, that of the crime of murder of which he was accused and at his trial acquitted, he was the guilty party and no one else but himself was engaged in the horrible transaction.'

But he could not face the same charge of murder a second time.

Young John, charming and jolly, and described as a man of pleasing manners, murdered his grandfather and endangered the lives of others. Had there been no suspicion of murder and had his father inherited, would Young John then have done away with him? And it was all for money. Ironically, at the last moment, George Bodle, having no faith in either his son or his grandson, changed his will and the money and property went to the female side of the family.

There might have been some truth in Mary Higgins's report of the conversation between Young John and his mother. If so, there may be a question about Mrs Bodle's part in all of this. There is a story that on her deathbed she exonerated her husband of any responsibility for the murder. So did she know all the time that her son was guilty?

Imponderables. There is not enough information available. But we do know that after the trial Young John Bodle went into business and failed. After that, he was employed by his brother-in-law, from whom he stole £80. For the next seven years or so there is nothing known of his whereabouts, though the suggestion is that he was in prison. The man is a mystery. He was chatting to the girls in the kitchen, making them laugh even while the water for the coffee was heating on the fire. And he knew that it was not only his grandfather who would drink it. Without a care, he played with the lives of several others who liked and trusted him.

Dangerously persuasive, Young John Bodle was a lethal companion in any kitchen, in any courtroom.

THE ARTIST

It was Richard Dadd's great good fortune to be born hugely gifted. And perhaps it was fortunate that this talent was encouraged by his father, Robert, who, after being a highly successful apothecary and chemist in Chatham High Street, and sharing his son's artistic flair, had started a new career as a gilder and carver. Father and son had so much in common. All through Richard's years at Rochester Cathedral Grammar School, his father paid for extra drawing lessons and in 1837 he began to pay his son's fees at the Royal Academy School of Art, where his teachers commented not only on the boy's artistic promise but also on his gentleness and cheerfulness. After finishing his studies Richard's professional career began as everyone expected. There were exhibitions at the Society of British Artists and at the Royal Academy. Commissions began to pour in for this most promising young artist. The father was proud and delighted at the boy's success, the son grateful for all the help he had received. And yet Richard Dadd was to murder his father.

In July 1842 Richard and his wealthy patron, Sir Thomas Phillips, set off on the Grand Tour. The great classical sites of antiquity – the Parthenon, the Baths of Caracalla, the amphitheatre at Nimes, the Pyramids – had been a source of wonder which had nourished poets and artists for the past two centuries and as the young artist travelled for ten months through France, Greece, Italy and the Middle East, he was inspired to complete very many paintings and drawings. But despite its charms and excitements the Grand Tour was an onerous business: the heat, the dust, the travel complications, the cumbersome coaches, the dubious accommodation and the reek of the bazaar, all made demands on the travellers. And Richard's health, despite his enthusiasm for all the new ideas and images that he was experiencing, began to suffer. At first his constant headaches were attributed to the effects of sunstroke but as Richard's condition increasingly deteriorated, Phillips became concerned about his young companion's state of mind, for he had begun to have delusions of the maddest kind.

Whether it was a result of Richard's mental disturbance or a cause of it is uncertain but in Egypt Richard was introduced to the hubble-bubble pipe. There is no information about what exactly he was smoking; whatever it was had a devastating effect upon him. He claimed to be receiving strange messages. At the start it was just the gurgling of the water in the pipe's tube that he said he heard but, as the days went on, the sounds turned into voices, telling him secrets that he had never suspected. It was Osiris, the ancient god of the Egyptians, who spoke to him and who, even after Richard left off smoking, would continue to speak to him through much of his life. Osiris, he believed, had chosen him.

After they left Egypt, Richard's mental frailty became more and more apparent. He was now convinced that it was the duty imposed upon him by his lord Osiris to oppose the Devil. He now believed that the Devil could take any shape, any form. By the time Richard reached Italy he was convinced that the Pope was the Devil. Had there not been a heavy Papal bodyguard Richard would have attempted to assassinate him at a public appearance in Rome. Weeks later, in May 1843, when they arrived in Paris, Richard attacked Phillips, another of those whom he now believed to be a manifestation of the Devil.

Before any serious harm occurred Richard was persuaded to return to London, where his father now lived. But there was a disappointment waiting for him. He had entertained high hopes of winning a prestigious national painting competition. The winner's works were to grace the Houses of Parliament. That his work was rejected just at this juncture in his life was a blow that further deepened the distress of this tortured man.

Whilst Richard's family were seriously concerned for him, in the way of many people when faced with such a domestic crisis, they thought optimistically that he would soon recover. What it was that ailed him would soon pass, they told themselves. But the weeks went by and there was no improvement. Eventually Robert Dadd could no longer ignore his son's bizarre behaviour and his assertions that he was engaged in a tireless struggle against the Devil. Reluctantly, Dr Alexander Sutherland of St Luke's Asylum was called in. His recommendation was that the young painter was 'non compos mentis' and that he should be confined.

But even with his doubts about his son confirmed, Dadd was unwilling to take the physician's advice. The thought of mental homes, their stigma, their sometimes barbarous routines, worried him deeply. He could not easily bring himself to place his son in such a place. And Richard in one of his more lucid intervals persuaded his father that all he required was rest in some quiet retreat away from the bustle of town. Why not go down to Kent where they had lived for so long, why not just relax down there? After all, it was summer and the countryside would be radiant. They could talk together, Richard told his father. It would be a chance, he said, to 'disburden' his mind.

On 28th August 1843, only a day or so after Dr Sutherland had been consulted, father and son travelled down to Cobham by gig, arriving at the Ship Inn in the early evening. The waiter was to recall Richard's rather surly manner when he served them. He had brought Robert a pot of tea and for Richard biscuits and cheese and a pint of porter. After an absence on other duties the waiter returned to the dining room to find that the younger Dadd had gone for a walk. His father had been invited to go with him but had excused himself. Robert told the waiter that he was rather tired. Noticing that the pint of porter had not been drunk the waiter asked, 'Doesn't your son like porter?' And wearily the old man answered, 'I don't know, I'm sure.' It was the tone of a desperate father, wondering perhaps if he should have followed the physician's advice.

Shortly after this, the waiter noticed that Richard had returned and, even later, he found that both men had left the inn. It was a pleasant summer's evening, a fine night for a stroll, he thought. Perhaps the old man had recovered from his tiredness. The waiter stayed up for them but by midnight, when they had not returned, he assumed that they had decided not to stay and had gone back home. Seeing the gig missing from the stable confirmed his belief.

Sometime after 7 am the following day, a Mr Lyter, a butcher, driving his gig through Cobham Park Road on his way to Wrotham market, saw what looked like a body lying about 40 yards from the roadside. He reined in his horse and climbed over a stile into the field where the corpse lay, the grass round about saturated with blood. He called to a shepherd tending his flock about two hundred yards away and asked him to watch over the corpse and then found a boy whom he sent with a message to the village constable. Lyter himself went to the Ship Inn. After all, he thought, this was a smartly dressed man, not a poor local.

Perhaps he was staying at the inn. But the waiter, hearing what Lyter had seen, immediately said, 'My God, that must be poor Mr Dadd,' and he accompanied the butcher to the scene of the crime where the constable was already in attendance.

Robert Dadd had been attacked on the edge of a deep hole surrounded by trees, known locally as Paddock Hole, though later it would be called Dadd's Hole. In the area round about there were indentations and scuffmarks on the ground, indicating a struggle. It was a good spot for a murder, just off the road, hidden by a hedgerow, a place that could have been chosen beforehand. Cobham Park Road was more of a lane, little frequented, with no houses nearby save for Cobham Hall. A robbery? Surely no robber would leave a gold watch, two sovereigns, 17 shillings in silver and a pair of silver mounted spectacles.

Dr Sanders from Gravesend had been summoned and he found a bruise on the left temple as if the victim had been dealt a severe blow. On the throat were two gashes, neither serious, which the doctor

Dadd's Hole, Cobham Park.

thought could have been caused accidentally in the course of a scuffle. The fatal blow was a stab to the left breast, which had penetrated a lung. There were two internal wounds from that stab wound as if the weapon had been partially drawn back after first entering the chest and after a twist of the blade another violent thrust had penetrated deep into the chest. Lying near the body was a spring-bladed knife and, underneath the victim, a cut-throat razor which had not been used.

The waiter informed the policeman that Robert Dadd's son had been with him. Where was he? Had the murderer done away with him too? For the next few hours there was a search for the young man. But then another member of the Dadd family came down to Cobham and the search for Richard Dadd, potential victim, became the search for Richard Dadd, murderer. The delay – no one's fault, for in Cobham they knew nothing of his problems – allowed Richard to disappear.

It later transpired that Richard was in London even before the body was discovered. He had taken the gig in which he and his father had travelled to Cobham. The police discovered that their quarry had visited Sol's Arms, a public house popular with artists in Hampstead Road. His extraordinary appearance and general manner, however, made the barmaid say that she thought 'the young gentleman was not in his right mind'. He had apparently heard that remark and had hurried away.

Further enquiries revealed that Richard had gone to his bank where he had drawn a large sum of money, which suggested that he intended to flee the country. He had then visited one of his friends at his rooms in Oxford Street. Here, he had talked about going to France. He had been wild-eyed and agitated and when the friend, sincerely concerned for him, tried to discover the reasons for such a hasty departure, Richard had become impatient and had promptly left with his queries unresolved. Even so, and in spite of this witness's information, it was not certain that he had gone abroad. There were some friends who were of the view that he had thrown himself into the Thames.

The same day, when police searched Richard's rooms in Newman Street, they found huge quantities of eggs and ale, the sole elements of the diet that he had recently obsessively followed. More disturbing were sketches of friends and acquaintances. Each one had a deep red gash across the throat.

A coroner's jury, sitting within hours of the discovery of the body, returned a verdict of 'wilful murder by some person or persons unknown'. But there was no doubt that Richard Dadd was responsible for the murder.

News of the horrific killing was in the newspapers within 24 hours. *The Times* had no doubt as to the culprit, a madman who had prevailed upon his father to go for a walk with him, all the time intending to take his life. Now there was the warning: 'Strong fears are entertained that he has some deadly weapon secreted about his attire, in order to protect himself from being captured.' The paper's 'own correspondent in Gravesend' related: 'A great many respectable persons at present sojourning at the town visited and inspected the spot this day, one of whom gave an involuntary shudder on approaching the place, where the blood of the victim was still apparent ... the stile, the top rail of which had been covered with boards until the jury met, still exhibited the stains of blood imprinted by the fingers of the murderer as he returned from the completion of his horrid work, and that way made his escape.'

From London Richard had managed to reach Dover where without difficulty he hired a boat to take him to Calais. *The Times* reported on 7th September, after he had been missing for a week: 'The son of the late Mr Robert Dadd still continues to elude the vigilance of his pursuers who have been despatched in all directions.' Two days later the *Illustrated London News*, under the headline 'Murder at Cobham Park', announced with disappointment, 'A rumour was prevalent during the week that the wretched parricide Dadd (the particulars of whose atrocity appeared in our later editions last week) had been arrested at Calais by one of the old Bow Street officers, on Monday last; but we regret to state that this is not the fact, and that the savage maniac is still prowling about in quest, perhaps, of other victims.'

But finally, on 11th September, the hunt was over although not before another dramatic event. The previous day the French newspaper, *Siècle*, had stated that Richard had drowned himself in France. But that report was then corrected: 'This last supposition is an erroneous one, for we have received at our office a visit from Monsieur Moyle, who, after reading the occurrence as we yesterday published it, had come to tell the following: Monsieur Moyle was [two evenings before] passing through the forest of Valence, near Montereau, and was seated in the coach by the side of a young Englishman, whose looks seemed to be wandering, and who had been for above a quarter of an hour amusing himself lowering Mr Moyle's cravat and collar. This singular practice provoked the traveller who desired his neighbour to have done with it; the latter then drew from his pocket an excellent English razor, and set about cutting the throat of the unfortunate Frenchman, who, despite a vigorous resistance, received four rather deep cuts. Notwithstanding his wounds, he succeeded in mastering the young man, whose madness seems to be a mania for cutting throats; for, on being taken before the justice of the peace at Montereau, he very quietly declared that his name was Richard Dadd, and that he had just recently arrived from England, where he had murdered his father by cutting his throat. But the most surprising circumstance of this strange story is, that the moment Richard Dadd was arrested he hastened to give all he had on him in order that his victim might be taken care of.'

On arrest, Richard was searched and in his pockets was found a list of people 'who must die'. It included Franz Ferdinand, the Emperor of Austria, and other prominent figures although Robert Dadd's name was still at the top of the list. Richard was instantly committed without trial to an asylum at Clermont.

Negotiations to have him returned to England were unduly protracted. Not until July 1844 were officers from Kent allowed to enter France to escort him back to face the magistrates' court in England.

Richard entered the courtroom at Rochester, heavily bearded and wearing a large, blue military cloak. He was pinioned by the arms. Charged formally by the chairman with the murder of his father, he shouted out angrily: 'You say I am the murderer, you bloody villain?'

'No doubt can remain in the mind of anyone who was present at the examination that the unfortunate young man is altogether irresponsible for his own acts,' commented the *Illustrated London News*. 'While in the presence of the bench his demeanour underwent various and instantaneous changes. The opinion of the bench was unanimous and decided as to the state of his mind, and there is little doubt that the last public scene in this melancholy tragedy has closed, and that this once promising artist will be removed to a place of permanent safe-keeping without coming to trial.'

Nevertheless, Richard Dadd made an appearance at Maidstone Assizes on 27th November 1844 where he was declared unfit to plead his case. He was sent to Bethlem Hospital in Southwark. He would stay there until 1863 when he was moved to the newly instituted Broadmoor

Robert Dadd at his easel in Bethlem Hospital, Southwark, 1856.

Hospital for the Criminally Insane where he would spend the rest of his days.

Even so, Richard was fortunate in that doctors at both hospitals recognised his quite remarkable and individual skill and encouraged him to continue painting. As a result the next 40 years were extremely successful in painting terms. His subjects were intriguing. He did not totally abandon the portraits and landscapes of his early professional years but now his work, surreal and fantastic, and minutely detailed, often included fairies and goblins and figures from Germanic folklore. His most famous painting is the mysterious and intricate *The Fairy Feller's Master Stroke*. In recent years, one of his canvases was brought for valuation to the Antiques Roadshow. It later sold for £105,000.

Richard Dadd died at Broadmoor in 1886 at the age of 69. It was the end of a tragic life shot through with blinding flashes of genuine fulfilment.

A SOLDIER'S JEALOUSY

Kind friends, come pay attention and listen to my song
It is about a murder, it won't detain you long
'Twas near the town of Folkestone this shocking deed was done
Maria and Sweet Caroline were murdered by Switzerland John.

('The Folkestone Murder' – folk song)

It was half past three on the Sunday morning, 3rd August 1856, when they set off from Albion Place, the two girls wearing light frocks, white socks and, over their shoulders, black cloaks against the morning's chill. As for Dedea Redanies, he was wearing the 'regimentals' of the British Swiss Legion – the peaked cap, the red jacket and the grey trousers with the red stripe. He must have looked dashing, the young soldier, with his two attractive companions.

Even so, though both she and her husband greatly liked Redanies because he was generally very courteous and pleasant, and because it was clear that he was going to marry 19-year-old Caroline, Mrs Back had been anxious about this walk all the way from Dover to Folkestone. Why wouldn't they take the train, she asked, when he broached the idea on Saturday evening? Caroline hadn't been well recently and her mother thought the eight-mile walk would be just too much for her. But Redanies had been insistent. A walk in the sunshine would be good for her, he said, ignoring the fact that there would be no sunshine for a good three hours after they set off. But if they took the train, Mrs Back argued, they would be able to leave later and enjoy whatever sunshine there was at Folkestone. The train was cheap enough. Redanies knew that, he told his prospective mother-in-law. It wasn't a matter of money. He'd plenty of money, he said. His sister had given him £100. But what if it rained, someone asked. He'd buy them parasols, Redanies replied, though where he might have bought them at the last minute on a Sunday was not explored.

The uniform of the British Swiss Legion, as worn by Redanies. (Courtesy of Landesmuseum, Zurich)

In that case, if they were walking, Maria would have to go with them, the concerned mother had said. And so it had been agreed. Sixteen-year-old Maria would accompany her sister in case she was unwell. She was pleased enough to do so. They were going to meet Redanies' wealthy sister who had come down from Aldershot. It was exciting. After all, they would all be related after Redanies and Caroline married. As for last night's argument about the portrait, which in a rage Redanies had broken up and thrown into the fire, that was over and done with. Just the sort of thing that happens, a lovers' tiff, no more than that. They had known each other for twelve months and the course of true love …

An hour or so later the trio was seen by a police constable. He remembered Dedea Redanies well enough. He had been in custody for having assaulted another policeman. This seems to have been out of character, for Redanies had generally a calm temperament. As things were to turn out, of course, there were occasions when his temperament was unstable.

At about five o'clock George Marsh, a labourer, met the soldier and the two girls on the road from Dover to Folkestone, all arm in arm, laughing and talking. Redanies had asked him the time in quite a cheerful manner. Some time afterwards, the ostler at the Royal Oak Inn, a mile or so east of Capel-le-Ferne, saw them and he, too, thought that they seemed at ease in each other's company. There was no further sighting of them.

It was midday, nine hours after the girls had left, when the Backs were called on at home. Their daughters, they were told, were dead. Their bodies were at a cottage about six miles away. And Dedea Redanies? No, he wasn't with them. He had last been seen at about seven o'clock, alone. He was running in the direction of Capel-le-Ferne. He appeared to be wearing a black cape.

The girls' bodies had been discovered at about nine o'clock at a desolate spot called Steddy Hole, just off the turnpike road. Today's maps call the area The Warren. Thomas Gurling, out for a stroll, had come across them. They lay about 14 yards apart across a footpath that led down to the sea. Gurling had raised the alarm, calling at the Valiant Sailor whose landlord had gone with him to remove the bodies to a nearby cottage.

Dr Bateman had come from Folkestone to examine the bodies. Both girls had numerous injuries. The cuts to her hands showed that Caroline had tried to defend herself but she had died from deep stab wounds to the chest, as had Maria. There was an immense loss of blood.

There was an immediate search for Redanies but he was not sighted until early on the Monday morning when, just after dawn, he was seen near Barham Downs. Sometime later, not having heard about the hue and cry, a woman at Broome Park gave him some bread and cheese. Then he arrived at Lower Hardres, calling on shopkeeper Elizabeth Atwood. She sold him two sheets of paper and, after he paid her, she agreed that he might stay to write some letters. Redanies was in Mrs Atwood's shop for one and a half hours, writing his letters, and she had some opportunity to observe him. In court, several months later, she recalled that the letters were in a foreign language. She also remembered that he had worn a red tunic and over it, a black cape. He had stuck his arms through the holes, wearing it rather like a waistcoat. Another cape he wore over his shoulders in the usual fashion. He had finally left her at about 10.30 am and had gone to the post office for stamps.

During the afternoon, PC George Fryer saw Redanies on the railway viaduct near Milton Chapel just outside Canterbury. He recognised him as the fugitive being sought by the police although the red tunic was by now discarded. The policeman approached Redanies to make an arrest but the soldier pulled out a knife and stabbed himself in the chest. Fryer was able to make his arrest and to staunch the heavy bleeding but Redanies had severely wounded himself and was not expected to live. In St Augustine's gaol in Canterbury he made a slow recovery. At one point he was given the last rites, so near was he to death.

So to our murderer, this apparently decent man, mild, inoffensive, by all accounts, if we gloss over the earlier assault charge on a policeman.

The Backs, poor but respectable and seemingly sensible folk, had accepted him into their family without any qualms. One evening a year earlier the rather good-looking Redanies had met the girls outside a theatre in Dover and had ever since been paying court to Caroline. The matter was never clarified but at one point in their courtship Redanies believed that she was pregnant by him.

Mrs Back and Caroline were laundresses and so, in order to give himself further opportunities to meet his lover, Redanies, a batman to Lt Schmidt, the regimental surgeon, used to take the lieutenant's laundry from Shorncliffe Camp, west of Folkestone, to their house in Dover ten miles away.

The Backs must have found the 26-year-old Dedea Redanies extremely interesting. Perhaps to these simple Dover folk he was exotic. He was a professional soldier, a mercenary, born in Serbia. He had travelled to the Middle East; had fought against the Austrians during the Hungarian revolution; had fought for them in their war against the Italian revolutionaries; had a horse shot from under him; had been twice decorated; and when the British, unable to recruit enough soldiers to fight in the Crimea, appealed for volunteers he had deserted the Austrians and in 1855 had joined the 2,000-strong British Swiss Legion stationed at Shorncliffe. There is no certainty about this but it is thought that he saw action in the Crimea.

Now, with some acquaintance with Italian, German and English in addition to his native Serbo-Croat, this highly regarded soldier was sometimes employed as an interpreter in the military hospital at Dover. That he was a Roman Catholic seems not to have concerned the Backs; perhaps they were simply astonished that this engaging young man had been born a Muslim, like most in Serbia, and had, during his time in Italy, converted to Catholicism.

Redanies was tried before Mr Baron Bramwell at Maidstone Assizes on 16th December 1856. He was excited, unhesitatingly pleading guilty to the murder of Caroline although not guilty to the murder of her sister. This rather startled the judge who feared that the admission of guilt would compel him to pass the death sentence without any evidence being heard. Perhaps there were exonerating circumstances, the judge said. The accused man ought to give himself a chance. His Lordship said he would not sentence him immediately but would give him a little time for reflection.

The British Swiss Legion at Shorncliffe camp 1855.
(Courtesy of M and M George)

The following day, with Redanies still proclaiming himself innocent of Maria's death, the judge, anxious that justice be done, announced that he felt that Redanies still had not understood his legal position. The judge said it would be more satisfactory for the trial to go forward and he appointed a barrister, Mr Barrow, to undertake the defence.

Redanies was now charged with the murder of Maria.

The motive for the murders was all too clear. Dedea Redanies was consumed with jealousy. He was deeply in love with Caroline, had thought they would marry but in recent weeks she had given him cause to doubt her faithfulness. One day when Redanies was in her house, an artilleryman had come down from an upstairs room. Caroline had told him that it was a friend and apparently Redanies had not pursued the matter. Then he had been posted to Aldershot and had written regularly to her. On his return he and Caroline were thumbing through the letters he had sent her. Among them Redanies came across a stray letter, which read: 'My dear Caroline, I shall soon have the pleasure of seeing you at Woolwich.' He had read that much when Caroline snatched the letter from him and had thrown it on the fire. A friend, Caroline had told Redanies, only a friend. Then on the Saturday, the day before the walk to Folkestone, she had returned his portrait – it might have been a photograph – an act that might have been construed as finishing the affair. But perhaps not. Whatever the reason, he had broken the frame and tossed it on the fire. And then she had told him that she was going to Woolwich. Of all places, Woolwich, where the letter writer was. Was she leaving Dover to go to that man? 'You no go to Woolwich,' he told her.

Now the exact sequence of events is hazy. Possibly the trip to Folkestone had been arranged earlier in the evening but it is more likely that there was a reconciliation. Perhaps Caroline cleared up the confusion, explaining that she was going to visit her elder sister Mary at Woolwich. Perhaps it was then that Redanies proposed the trip to Folkestone to meet his sister. When Redanies left the house – and there is even some doubt as to where he slept that night – was it Albion Place or Dover barracks? – the girls were preparing for the next day's walk. And Redanies went to a cutler's in town and bought a knife with a four-inch blade. There was no sister coming to meet the girls. He had invented that story.

So there was the motive – a deep, corrosive jealousy, which Redanies had concealed perhaps for weeks from the four members of a family that genuinely trusted and liked him.

The two letters that Redanies wrote while on the run make especially compelling reading. It is important to recall that they were written by a desperate man, lonely, in a foreign land, guilty only 24 hours earlier of a terrible double murder. How could he clearly express what had happened when his emotions were so turbulent, when he had destroyed the life of his lover and her sister? And then we recall too that these letters were originally written not in his own language but in imperfect German for he realised there would be no Serbo-Croat translator near at hand and his grasp of English did not extend to writing it. But here they are, the first addressed to Mrs Back and the second to Lt Schmidt:

Dearest Mother Back – On the first lines I pray to forgive the awful occurrence to the unlucky Dedea Redanies which I committed on my very dear Caroline and Maria Back yesterday morning at five o'clock. I perpetrated the horrible deed. Scarcely am I able to write, my heart breaks for my ever memorable Caroline and Maria. The cause of this deed is – 1. I heard that Caroline is not in the family way as I first believed. 2. Because Caroline intends to go to Woolwich. 3. That I cannot stay with my very dear Caroline; it made my heart so confused till at last the unhappy thought came into my head that Caroline rather may die from my hands than to allow Caroline's love being bestowed upon others. However, I did not intend to murder also Maria, her sister; but not having other opportunity, and as she was in my way, I could not do otherwise than stab her too. Dear Mother Back – Saturday evening, when I came I had not the least idea of this awful act; but as I heard that my dear Caroline gave me back my likeness [the portrait], and as she told me she would leave, I did not know any other way in my heart-break than to go to the cutler, and I bought a poniard which divided the hearty lovers. Arm in arm I brought both my dearest souls in the world over to the unlucky place near the road before Folkestone, and requested them to sit down; but the grass being wet they refused to do, and I directed then Caroline to go forward, and I went behind Maria, into whose breast I ran the dagger. With a dull cry she sank down, and with a most broken heart I rushed then upon Caroline, lifting the poniard in my hand towards her. 'Dear Dedea,' cried she with a half-dead voice, and fell down with weeping eyes. Then I rushed over her, and gave her the last kisses as in everlasting remembrance. I could not live a more dreadful hour in my life than that was; and from my broken heart I know not where my senses were, and I took as a lasting keepsake both the black shawls of Maria and my dear Caroline as a mourning suit for me, leaving the awful spot with weeping eyes and a broken heart.

Never shall I forget my dear Caroline and Maria, and the poniard remains, covered with blood of my dear Maria and Caroline, with me until it will pierce my own heart, and I shall see again my dear Maria and Caroline in the eternal life.

Farewell, and be not troubled about the blissfully deceased angels of God; and forgive the unhappy, ever weeping,

Dedea Redanies.

Is this the letter of a sane man?

The second letter, addressed to Lieutenant Schmidt, reads:

Dearest Mr Lieutenant Schmidt,
With weeping eyes I beg you to forgive unfortunate Dedea, and I let you know in short that it was not my intention to steal your watch. I only lent it to the sister of Caroline, when Maria will give it you back, if you will be kind enough to go to Dover to fetch it under the said address – 'Miss Maria Back, 5 Albion Place, Dover.' At the same time, I enclose the ticket belonging to Dr Baumgarten and let him know that I have not received the watch. I am sorry that I cannot put the money in because I have spent it. Dearest Mr Lieutenant Schmidt, keep the portrait and the hair to remember forever that fearful Sunday when both girls whom I shall never forget with trouble and pleasure. Dearest Mr Lieutenant Schmidt, I thank you for all the kindness which I have received from you; and forgive the unfortunate Dedea Redanies, who is ready every minute to be arrested, and the same dagger which murdered my only friend shall murder myself. I have written to the mother of Caroline a letter. Be kind enough to let her know what has happened, and go to Dover and interpret it for her. You are very kind and I am thankful.

Dedea Redanies.

There is incoherence in this letter, scribbled in Mrs Attwood's shop. We know nothing of the lieutenant's watch or of Dr Baumgarten's ticket. And what of the reference to Miss Maria Back? She is dead and he knows that. Is this some further aberration? Later he would plead not guilty to her murder. It is now beyond explanation. But we can guess at the man's state of mind.

And it was this, his state of mind, which might in the end have cleared Dedea Redanies of a murder charge. Was he insane? At least, was he insane at the time of the murder? That he was deeply disturbed by the enormity of his actions cannot be doubted.

In court, Mr Barrow, for the defence, pleaded that as the prisoner's advocate he had had no instructions from a solicitor and was unable to communicate with his client. He reminded the jury that it was obvious that Redanies, who had pleaded guilty, was quite indifferent to the result and this supported the notion that he was not responsible when he committed the murders. Although jealousy had been suggested as the reason for the killings, Mr Barrow believed that the girls had been murdered on impulse. This sudden impulse, he said, was well understood by medical men and known in medical jurisprudence under the name of 'homicidal monomania', an uncontrollable and sudden impulse. Therefore, Mr Barrow claimed, the jury would be justified in acquitting the prisoner on grounds of insanity.

In his summing up, the judge posed these questions. Did Redanies know the nature of the act he was committing and was he aware that it was a wrongful act? For if the answers to both questions were in the affirmative, it would be their duty to say he was guilty.

After a short withdrawal, the jury returned a verdict of guilty.

Addressing Redanies through an interpreter, the judge said that the crime did not appear to have been committed from any feeling of revenge or to obtain possession of any property or from any other hateful feelings. 'Although, therefore, one may pity you more, it is necessary to make an example as much in this as in any other case of murder.' Redanies had been induced to commit the crime simply by allowing his bad passions to prevail. His offence was therefore equally hateful and equally deserving of the supreme punishment.

In the condemned cell Redanies was visited by Mrs Back. He begged forgiveness and ultimately she forgave him. Did she suspect that he was not responsible for his actions? Certainly Father Lawrence, a Catholic priest who visited him daily, was quite certain that the man was insane, claiming constantly that he had not murdered the Back sisters but had simply sent them on to Heaven before him. He knew they would be there, waiting for him. Drawings he did at the time follow the same theme, showing him and the girls in some blissful paradise. The priest believed that Redanies was totally deluded and he wrote to the Home Secretary asking for a reprieve. He was unsuccessful.

From his cell Redanies wrote a letter to the Backs to be opened after his death. It further indicates his frame of mind.

Dear Parents,
Forget your anger against me and do not curse me in your grave. Remember that by doing so you would not only afflict me but also my dear Caroline and Maria. They love me as I love them. We are

above with our Father again together, where we shall see one another again and live forever with the Father of love, Jesus Christ. I greet you with my dear Caroline and Maria, and wish you the blessings of God and prosperity until the voice of God calls you, too, to life everlasting.'

(signed) Caroline Back, Dedea Redanies, Maria Back.

And so to the final grim scene.

The dismal bell is tolling, for the scaffold I must prepare.
I trust in heaven my soul shall rest and meet dear Caroline there.
Now, all young men, take warning from this sad fate of mine.
To the memory of Maria Back and lovely Caroline.

Thus goes the last verse of the old folk song. On 1st January 1857 Dedea Redanies was executed on top of the porter's lodge at Maidstone gaol, the first execution there for seven years. He appeared little concerned about what was about to happen to him. The newspapers report that he walked with 'a cheerful step'. On the scaffold he announced, 'In a few moments I shall be in the arms of my dear Caroline. I care not for death.'

The 5,000 people attending met with the approval of the authorities: 'As exemplifying the remarkably good character of the crowd, we are informed that not one single complaint of robbery has reached the ears of the police.' It seems appropriate that poor, deluded Dedea Redanies should have left this earth with some degree of respect.

4

LIKE FATHER ...

Mary Atkins was terrified. She was used to the arguments, to the shouting, to the bruises she had seen on her mother's arms. It had been going on for the past two years in their little West Malling cottage, a cramped place, where there was nowhere to hide from violence. Mary she had seen how her mother had suffered, had seen how her father raged. But today it was different, more frightening. Only a minute earlier Mary had gone downstairs when she heard her mother 'squeak', just to see what it might be. When she went through the kitchen and into the washhouse, there was her father in a real state. He had a knife in his hand. And what can an 11-year-old do in such circumstances? She had taken to her heels and dashed next door to Mr Ridley's but for all her hammering on the door and for all her shouting, there was no reply. And so she went back home. What else could she do? But now the kitchen door was locked. What was happening? She began banging on the door, calling out to be let in. But there was no reply. She went to the window. She saw her mother lying on the floor, her father bending over her, the knife to her throat. Mary ran off again. Perhaps she might get help from the Woolletts, their other neighbours, but only the three children were in that house so there was no help there. And next she thought she would try Mrs Woodger. Surely somebody could help.

Shortly after this, only a minute or two later, Ann Smith, Mr Ridley's housekeeper, heard what she was to describe as a scratching at the door. And crying, too. Why she hadn't answered young Mary's earlier knocking and calling out is not clear. These were modest two-up, two-down cottages. It wasn't as though Mrs Smith was at the far end of a mansion. Perhaps she hadn't heard. Or perhaps by the time she went to the door Mary, in desperation, had gone off home again. But when she heard the scratching and the crying, she opened the door and found Mary's mother, Betsy Atkins, staggering away. She was, as Mrs Smith said, 'all over blood'. She went to see what help she could offer but now

John Atkins appeared. He raised the knife, threatening her, and she was afraid for herself and could only watch as the injured woman made her unsteady way across the lane and into the clover field.

Robert Pearch, working in one of the nearby hop gardens, heard some kind of commotion and, when he went to investigate, found Betsy in the field. She was conscious but did not recognise him. 'Who is it?' she asked.

Realising that he could do nothing to help, Pearch sent for a doctor and called for assistance from the neighbours. Then he saw Atkins at his back door and went to him. Atkins asked Pearch how his wife was, though not with any real concern for her welfare. After telling him how grave her condition so obviously was, Pearch asked Atkins what had happened. Whatever had happened, Atkins replied, not going into any detail, it served her right.

By the time Dr Pope arrived Betsy Atkins was already dead. She had two throat wounds and a stab that had pierced the jugular vein. Atkins had been by now arrested and taken to the Malling lock-up.

The following morning, Superintendent Hulse of the Malling Division went to speak to the prisoner. Atkins greeted him with, 'Good morning. Is the woman dead?' Told that she was, he said to the Superintendent, 'I did it. I saw Barton looking through the window and, had he come in, it would have been prevented. I have seen Barton and my wife in bed together. I am very sorry for what has happened but it is now too late.'

A desperate man, then. A deceived husband, driven to murder at the thought of his wife in the arms of another man. Another of those age-old tales, what the French call a 'crime passionel'. Or so it might have seemed to those who did not know the facts of the case.

When 42-year-old John Atkins from Malling faced trial at the Kent Assizes at Maidstone in July 1861 the court heard a distressing, tragic tale. True enough, over the past two years, there had been constant arguing, often long into the night. The neighbours could not avoid knowing what went on in the Atkins' household, the rows, the penetrating cries, the shouts, the blows.

One Sunday about two weeks before the murder, John Ridley had heard screaming from the Atkins' cottage. He had gone to see what was the matter. He had looked through the window and there was Betsy sitting at the bottom of the stairs, hysterical, in tears. She appeared to be half-naked. Atkins was holding her gown and shawl. Ridley shouted through the window, asking what was wrong but neither of those inside could hear him. Then Atkins had come outside to speak to him. He was carrying a knife. He couldn't go on living with Betsy, he said. It was all too much for him. Ridley had come up with a glib solution. Why didn't Atkins just leave her, he asked. Atkins had said that he had a great mind to run away but that he did not want to leave his children. At this point, Betsy had come out of the house, dressed once more, and the conversation between the two men came to a sudden end when Atkins went to her, seized her by the arm, and led her back inside. Once there, he tore off her dress and threw it on the fire. Ridley did not explain what happened after that but it must be assumed that the fracas continued and the whole village knew the details of all that had occurred.

Just a week before the murder Atkins had been to Peckham, staying the week with his brother Tom and his wife. Mrs Atkins told how her brother-in-law had arrived unexpectedly early on the morning of 7th July. Obviously distressed, he told them that he had been running away from the police all night. He said that his wife had been to the police about him and that if he were to be caught he would be locked up for life.

Throughout his stay at Peckham, Atkins suffered from headaches and he was frequently depressed. There were times when he would go into a corner of the room and stand listening to the voices that he was convinced spoke to him. At mealtimes he would come to the table and take his food and then disappear to eat it elsewhere. He would sit in a chair at other times, praying for up to half an hour, begging that God would take him. One day when his brother Tom was out of the house, Atkins announced that Tom had been killed 'up against a gate across a meadow'. When his brother arrived home later, Atkins was surprised to see him. 'I thought you was dead, Tom,' he said. But it was Betsy who had taken his life away, he would say. And the old sexual jealousy, the delusion of the woman's unfaithfulness, would crop up time and again. It was all the fault of George Barton from Town Malling: he had found him in bed with his wife. This is what he constantly said, what he firmly believed.

During Atkins' absence from home, another neighbour, Mary Stevens, had been to visit Betsy. No sooner had Mrs Stevens arrived than Betsy had fainted and their subsequent conversation suggested that she was exhausted by the constant quarrelling. Mrs Stevens spoke of the bruises on Betsy Atkins' arms and the endless arguing that had been going on for the past two years. When Betsy's uncle had come to stay with them for a while Atkins had become convinced that she and her uncle had had a sexual relationship.

Only an hour before the murder, Hester Ifield had called at the house and had found Atkins sitting by the fire and Betsy writing a letter. Atkins told her his head had been very bad all day. Betsy had been up with him for much of the night.

Such was the tale told at the trial of John Atkins, who in the end was declared unfit to plead and was sent to a mental hospital. But what can have been the effect on poor Mary and her other sister? And what about the effect upon 15-year-old Tom Atkins, the only son?

Impossible to say but young Tom, twelve years after his father's trial for murder, also found himself at the Assizes on a charge of murder.

Early in the morning of Sunday, 24th August 1873, Samuel Stone, a bricklayer, going to work along the Snodland-Malling turnpike road, noticed quite obvious signs of a bloody scuffle in the road. And clearly someone else, William Imms, had seen the signs because he was already peering round, looking into a turnip field. Then the two men came across a body, fearfully battered, bloodied, mangled, not 20 feet from the road.

The corpse of a well-built man was stretched out nearly at full length, one leg slightly drawn up, an arm extended as if to protect the head. The face was smashed in, the features indistinguishable, the head shattered to pieces, the brains protruding, portions of it scattered over the ground.

The dead man wore a police uniform though at first that was scarcely obvious, so covered was it in mud. The officer's helmet lay some feet away from the body. His truncheon was nowhere to be found and it was assumed by Superintendent Hulse, still with the Malling Division, that it must have been the murder weapon. The policeman's watch had stopped at 2.40 am, presumably during the savage struggle that had taken place.

There was little in the way of clues to the assailant's identity although he had left a bloodied cap in the hedge. The wretched victim on the other hand, despite the savage beating he had taken, was too readily recognised. It was PC Israel May, the local policeman. Whoever had overcome this father of three must have been of phenomenal strength unless, as the *Kent and Sussex Courier* opined, May had been surprised by 'his barbarous assailant'. The policeman was extremely powerfully built.

The body was taken to the Bull at Malling where the local surgeon carried out the post-mortem. He found a large wound on May's forehead and a larger one at the back. It was one, or both, of these blows that had proved fatal but there were other injuries. The constable's nose was broken and his left cheek was shattered. He had bled from the left eye and ear. There was severe bruising on the right elbow as though he had attempted to deflect a blow to the head.

The inquest held at the Bull on the Monday produced a verdict of wilful murder by a person or persons unknown. But were there any possible suspects? There was talk of a couple of Royal Engineers in the area and they needed to be found. They had been staying at the Nag's Head but had now left for London. While the enquiries about the two soldiers were being made, Superintendent Hulse continued talking to local people, trying to piece together PC May's last hours.

At 10.45 pm on the Saturday night the constable had been seen talking to a man slumped against the wall of the Bull, apparently incapable of walking. May had advised him to go home but there had been an altercation, in which the two Royal Engineers had been involved. What part they had played and whose side they had taken is unclear but the situation cannot have been too serious for May shortly went on his way to deal with another minor emergency in the village, leaving the drunk still propped against the pub wall.

Shortly afterwards the drunk and the two soldiers, as they later testified, had left the public house together, walking towards Ham Hill. But finally it was too much for the drunken man who fell down in the road and, despite the best efforts of his companions, he could not be roused. And so he was left at the roadside to sleep it off. Shortly afterwards at about eleven o'clock May had come upon the man's recumbent form and had tried to rouse him, with no success. He had left him where he had found him and had continued his patrol.

PC May was last seen alive at Ham Hill, a mile or so from the scene of the crime. At about 1.30 am he had spoken briefly to Mrs Selina Upton, wife of a local beer-house keeper, and had then gone on towards Snodland.

The involvement of the two soldiers was soon clarified. They were picked up in Whitechapel and returned to Snodland where they gave an account of their night out, after which they were discharged for lack of direct evidence.

But now it was the drunk, a local man, 27-year-old Thomas Atkins, who was being sought, though how a man so profoundly inebriated could have got the better of a supremely fit and strong man like Israel May was a matter of some surprise.

Edward Baker, the ferryman at Snodland had informed Hulse that on the Saturday evening sometime after eight o'clock he had ferried Thomas Atkins over the river from Burham where he lodged. According to the ferryman, Atkins was already inebriated and uttering threats about what he intended to do when he met the constable. There was a history between the two men for Atkins had been arrested more than once by May for disorderly behaviour when under the influence.

But if Atkins was now the suspect he was nowhere to be found. He had left his lodgings at about eight o'clock on the Saturday evening, telling his landlord that he expected to be back at about eleven but he had not been seen since. Nor on the Monday had he turned up at the local cement works where he was employed as a labourer. A reward of £100 for information leading to his arrest was now offered.

It was not until Friday that the police had any clue as to the missing man's whereabouts. On the previous Tuesday, three children, gleaning in a wheat field, had seen a man with a bandaged head in Birling Trees Wood, no more than a mile from Snodland. He had run into the open across a clearing to a smaller wood. Although at the time they had thought his actions strange, they had not realised that he was being sought by the police and consequently had not thought about telling anyone about what they had seen. Only on the Friday had they the slightest idea that the man was a fugitive and only then had they reported it.

By the time the police searched the wood Atkins was nowhere to be seen. But May's missing truncheon was found there. This was another indication that the police were seeking the right man.

On Saturday, 30th August Superintendent Hulse received a telegram from a policeman stating that Atkins had been seen that morning at the Horse and Groom in Stansted and that he was now on the road to West Kingsdown. Shortly after this a local policeman came upon the wanted man sitting on the side of the road. Atkins was arrested and put up no resistance. He was worn out and starving and he asked the policeman if he would give him some of the bread and cheese he had in his pocket.

At first, when he was hiding in the wood, Atkins said, a man had given him some food but since then he had not had eaten. His clothing was heavily stained. He had tried to wash out the marks of blood but had had little success. Some stains he had tried unsuccessfully to get rid of by rubbing them with chalk.

Atkins was taken to Malling where he was charged with murder, yet it must have been a puzzle to Superintendent Hulse how this man of quite slim build and shorter than PC May by several inches had managed to overcome the sturdy policeman. But Atkins' previous work as a bargeman, pulling barges along the river, had developed his arms and hands, giving him a quite abnormal strength. Even drunk he had been able to outfight the constable.

Atkins was charged with murder by Superintendent Hulse. Shortly afterwards he asked if he might speak once more to the Superintendent, who went to the cell where the prisoner was held. Atkins was warned that anything he might say could be used as evidence at the trial but Atkins insisted that he wished to give his version of what had occurred. He expressed regret at what he had done but said he had had no idea he had killed PC May. He did not deny that he had fought the policeman but he resolutely rejected any suggestion that he had set out to kill him. Indeed it was not his fault, he said. He hadn't started the fight. He had, he admitted, struck May on the head half a dozen times but it was in response to what he claimed was a violent blow to his own head.

At his trial before Mr Baron Pigott at Maidstone in December 1873, Atkins' statement in prison to Superintendent Hulse was central to his defence. 'I was lying along by the road', he said, 'and the constable came and shook me. I got up and the constable then struck me on the head with his staff and made the wound you see here [pointing to a contusion on his head]. We struggled together and fell through the hedge into a field. We continued to struggle there, and I took the constable's staff from him and hit him about the head. I threw the staff away, I don't know where. I should not have done it if the constable had not interfered with me. That is the truth, so help me God.'

There was no conclusive forensic proof that Atkins had been in a bloody struggle with the policeman. His clothing had been sent to Dr Thomas Stevenson, at the Royal College of Physicians. After examining the garments the doctor stated that 'the blood might be that of an

The attack on PC May at Snodland, as depicted in the
Illustrated Police News, *September 1873.*

ordinary domestic animal. It is impossible in the present state of science
to distinguish with certainty between the blood of a human being and
that of an ordinary domestic animal.'

But the nub of the case was not about such evidence. It rested on who
struck the first blow. It was the defence case that the wound on Atkins'
head was consistent with his account that the constable struck him first.
The defence did not dispute the fact that the accused had used the
constable's truncheon; in fact, that served as proof that he had not
sought out May, ready prepared with a weapon to assault him. As for
the witnesses who spoke of hearing Atkins making threats to deal with
the policeman, these, the defence claimed, were made by a drunken
man. What had happened, Atkins' counsel declared, had not been
premeditated. The defence alleged that the evidence against Atkins

would not support a charge of wilful murder but it was accepted that it was consistent with manslaughter.

In his summing up Mr Baron Pigott directed the jury to concentrate on one question: did the accused set out with the deliberate intention of taking the life of PC May? They were to bear in mind that the only occasion on which he had shown malice against the policeman was when he was drunk. The words uttered by a man in drink, the judge pointed out, had not always to be taken at face value. They might be regarded as no more than empty threats.

That the weapon had been wrested from the constable was significant, said the judge. This indicated that Atkins had not furnished himself with a weapon beforehand, which might show that there was no premeditation. Finally, he directed the jury to consider whether Atkins was telling the truth when he said that PC May had struck him first. If the accused was telling the truth, then the constable had committed an unlawful act. In his Lordship's opinion that would be material when the jury came to consider their verdict.

Of course the court had also heard about Atkins' father and about other members of his family, a grandfather and an aunt, both of unsound mind. These were undoubtedly important elements that the jury members carried with them into their deliberations.

After 20 minutes, the jury returned a verdict of guilty of manslaughter. Asked if he wished to say anything before sentence was passed, Atkins expressed his remorse, repeating that it had not been his intention to kill PC May.

In passing sentence, the judge expressed his strong disapproval of any resistance to an officer under any circumstance even though that officer might be exceeding his duty. He said the jury had believed Atkins' statement the policeman had struck him first and that mitigated in some degree the seriousness of the offence. He could not but believe, however, that Atkins had continued to rain blows upon May's head long after he must have known that he was seriously, if not mortally, wounding the policeman. It was, he said, an aggravated case of manslaughter.

Thomas Atkins was sentenced to 20 years' penal servitude. He served fifteen years, after which he emigrated to the United States. Like that more unfortunate man, his father, he had escaped the gallows.

Israel May, a very popular policeman, was buried in Snodland churchyard. A huge procession followed the coffin from the Bull where the body lay. At his funeral service the rector reminded the mourners that 'few can imagine what dangers a policeman has to face, while his fellow creatures safely sleep.'

An appeal fund was raised later in which the rector wrote of the constable, 'he was a man as good as he was brave ... It needs to be known that his widow is in every way worthy of a devoted husband.'

The officer's memorial stone reads: 'In memory of Israel May aged 37 years. Police Constable of the Malling Division, Kent County Constabulary. Found cruelly murdered on Sunday morning August 24th 1873. Erected by voluntary contributions. The Memory of the Just is Blessed.'

5

ON THE WAY BACK
FROM THE PUB

It was sometime after eight o'clock, the light was fading and George Turk was escorting his lady friend, the widow Mrs Naomi Connor, back along the footpath from Maypole to her home in Herne Street. It was a pleasant stroll on a May evening, with fields under the plough and pasture on either side of them, with the hedges blossoming and deep calm settled on the land. The early summer sounds, birds on the wing, lowing cows, a distant bleating of sheep, were broken only by an indistinct noise ahead of the couple. As they came closer it was more like a moaning that they heard or perhaps a kind of sighing. It came from just beyond them, just off the pathway. And then George Turk spotted the body, lying in a ditch. Mrs Connor saw him too and screamed, turning back, away from the stricken man. But Turk was concerned for him, his bloodied face so grossly disfigured, the forehead dented, the right eye out of its socket, the cheek bones, the nose, the mouth battered out of shape, the blood still oozing from the wounds. Turk tried to raise the injured man but it was futile and so he laid his head down again into the ditch bottom with its mélange of blood, bone and brain.

And now only slowly did George Turk realise that the wrecked figure he was trying to assist was someone whom he had known for years: it was Richard Steed from Maypole. Yet so devastating was the damage to the face that Steed was recognisable only by his clothes and particularly by his familiar red muffler. All that Turk could do now was to seek help and, comforting the distressed Mrs Connor as they went, he returned to the village. Along the way they met a man called Petts and Turk asked him to stand guard over Steed and to do what he could for him. After that, the first call in the village was to the Steed home, to tell the family what had occurred. Straightaway, 11-year-old Albert Steed hitched up the cart and took his mother and Turk to where his father lay. Between them they managed to lift the dying man into the cart and take him home where his married daughter, Julia, knew her father only by his clothing and his hands.

Shortly after ten o'clock Dr Jameson arrived from Sturry but Richard Steed, lying in the front room of his house, was already dead, the victim of a ferocious attack. His skull appeared to have been fractured by some heavy instrument and there were, the doctor noted, indentations on the face that suggested he had been stamped on by someone wearing hob-nailed boots.

At the inquest on Monday, 4th May 1863, Dr Jameson described the extent of the injuries, saying quite matter-of-factly: 'I put the features together and recognised the deceased.' He could do little more.

But what motive can there have been? Who was so incensed that he felt not only that he must give Steed a beating but that he should make it so brutal, so final? At no point had Steed, husband of Hannah and father of Julia, Albert and three younger children, made an enemy of anyone who hated him enough to deprive him of his life. He was a hard working 55-year-old, typical of many working-class Victorians in that he turned his hand to a variety of tasks. He was a general dealer and carrier, using his cart to trundle sacks, boxes and crates of anything that needed to be moved in a radius of perhaps a dozen miles or so. There is even a suggestion that he sometimes delivered letters but at the time of his death his principal activity was the little business he ran from a stall beside the railway line then being constructed from Herne Bay to Margate. The navvies working along the line always had need of drinks and sandwiches and trade seems to have been brisk.

On the day of his death, Saturday, 2nd May, Steed had been working at the railway as usual. His son

The Street, Hoath, R. Willis 1908.

Albert said later in the magistrates court, 'I was with my father at Boggs Hole between Herne and Reculver on Saturday. He was selling coffee and small beer to the men employed on the railway works. About three o'clock my father went towards the pay office and I went home with the cart.' That was the last time he spoke to his father.

Early on the Sunday morning Superintendent William Walker, accompanied by Sergeant Gower, both from Canterbury, went to Maypole and examined the body. He also spoke to members of the family, gleaning important information from Albert about money in his father's possession on the Saturday afternoon. After this, the two officers made their way to the crime site, midway between Maypole and Ridgeway Farm on the southern edge of Herne. At the magistrates' court, Walker was to describe what he found. 'There was a round indent in the ground, about two or three inches deep, as if a man's head had been pummelled into the ground. There was another mark, as if the heel of a boot had been struck into the ground. There were no marks of a struggle having taken place.' But there was, he told the court, a large quantity of blood and brain.

There were several people ready to aid the policemen in their investigation. Steed had left the railway at about 6.20 pm and had come into the Prince Albert in Herne Street shortly after seven o'clock. He had sat drinking for a while with some of the navvies whom he knew and, after half an hour or so, had left for home in the company of another man, Alfred Eldridge. Witnesses recalled Steed saying to Eldridge, 'Are you going home? We'll go along together.'

Sometime later, the two men were seen 'going along very friendly together'. Another witness, Isaac Pooley, working in the garden of his cottage in Albion Lane at Herne, spoke to Steed and although he did not recognise his companion, he did remember that he wore a brown, thigh-length coat which was darned at the elbow and had a patch on the back of its neck. He said that the men were making for the path that led through the fields to Maypole.

Later that evening, Eldridge was seen emerging onto the road from the footpath at Millbank as though he had come from Herne by the more northerly of the two possible footpaths. He had then called in for a loaf at the Maypole bake house, where Mrs Saunders found him quite his usual self and they had chatted together for some minutes. Eldridge already owed the baker three shillings but this evening he handed over two shillings to pay off some of the debt. This would be another piece of information that helped to convince the policemen that Eldridge merited serious consideration for they knew already that money in Steed's possession during the afternoon was missing when his body arrived home in the evening. Albert Steed had told them that on the Saturday afternoon his father counted out in front of him nine shillings and ninepence in his possession. He had then put the silver coins in his right-hand trouser pocket and the copper in the left. In the evening when the body was brought home there was only sixpence in silver and fourteen pence in copper in his pockets. Steed would have spent no more than twopence or threepence on beer in the Prince Albert pub, and there was no accounting for where the rest of his money had gone. And perhaps by now the policemen had heard about another of Eldridge's debts. He owed money to Richard Steed.

By ten o'clock Superintendent Walker and Sergeant Gower were at the cottage near Hoath church where 32-year-old Alfred Eldridge lived with his wife and four-month-old child. The man they sought was very powerful looking, a former soldier who had served in the Crimea and in India during the mutiny. Yes, of course he knew Steed, he told the officers. He and his wife had lodged in his house some months earlier. He said that he had just heard from a neighbour, only an hour or so earlier, that Steed had had some sort of accident but he knew nothing more about it.

Walker asked to see the clothing that Eldridge had worn the previous evening. The overcoat was patched and darned just like the one worn by the stranger Pooley had seen with Steed. Eldridge's trousers were clearly stained with mud and blood. There was staining on his vest as well. Walker noticed that he was wearing shoes and clean socks. Where were the boots he was wearing the day before, the navvy was asked. And would he let them see the socks he wore yesterday, too? Eldridge brought the boots out of a cupboard. It was obvious to the policemen that they had been washed and dried, but they had not been cleaned thoroughly enough. They still bore traces of mud, hair, thin strands of red wool, and some brownish stains, which had not been removed. And the socks? Eldridge hesitated over this, suggesting at first that he was still wearing them but Gower would not accept this answer. The socks Eldridge had on were too clean. He couldn't have been working on the railway line in those the day before. After Eldridge said that the socks were somewhere in the house, the policemen looked for them but failed to find them. During this search of the cottage and the inspection of the clothing, Eldridge admitted to Sergeant Gower that for the last four months he and Steed had been in dispute over a debt.

Eldridge was asked which route he had taken home on the Saturday night. He explained that he and Steed had left the Prince Albert together but had left each other before reaching Pooley's cottage in Albion Lane. Earlier their path divided and he had taken the left-hand fork while Steed had gone along the parallel path towards Ridgeway Farm where he was later found. Walker and Gower then accompanied Eldridge along the route that he claimed to have followed but it was even longer and less direct than the policemen had been led to believe. As Walker was to tell the magistrates the next day, 'His proper way home from Maypole Street led by Ridgeway Farm and by the place where the murder was committed.' The policeman did not believe Eldridge's claim that they had separated before reaching Pooley's house. Walker now arrested Eldridge on suspicion of murder.

At the conclusion of the inquest held in the Admiral Rodney at Hoath the jury returned a verdict of wilful murder. The coroner stated that in 30 years he had never seen a more brutal and diabolical killing. It was

The Prince Albert, Herne, c.1930. (Courtesy Herne Bay Library)

a case that was to gain great local notoriety and the magistrates' court hearing was crowded, as was the street outside.

There was little attempt by the press to conceal Eldridge's background or its own conviction of the man's guilt before ever the case went to trial at the Assizes. The *Kentish Gazette* announced that 'his features are somewhat sharp and there is something sinister in his appearance though the cast of his countenance is not repulsive.' This, of course, was at the time when it was believed that criminals were identifiable by their facial characteristics. Furthermore, 'the prisoner bears a very indifferent character and some time ago he was convicted, before the City Justices at Canterbury, of stealing wood and underwent three months' imprisonment.' And whilst it was true that Eldridge had been in the army for twelve years, the *Gazette* confided, he had been discharged 'without a character'. Penalty points already against the accused even before he set foot in the dock.

At the magistrates' court Eldridge's bloodstained trousers and vest were presented in evidence. He claimed that these had been stained in the course of his work. One of the magistrates, Captain Ruxton, put a question to Mrs Steed about the colour of her husband's hair. It was grey and black, she told him. 'It is not a question of identity,' Ruxton replied to the chairman, who had queried the relevance of the question, 'but as to the weapon with which the man was killed. The prisoner's boot had hairs of that colour adhering to it.'

The court was suddenly startled by the introduction of fresh evidence about the murder weapon. An iron ploughshare had been found near the spot where the murder had been committed. Richard Larkin, the blacksmith at Maypole, had sent a written statement to the court which said, 'Yesterday afternoon my wife told me there was a plough some distance in the field and as Mr Jameson said the murder had been committed by some powerful instrument, it struck me that such an instrument as the point of a plough might have been used. I therefore went to the plough this morning, and took this point from it, as there appeared to be stains of blood on it. The plough was about 150 yards from the place where the murder was committed and the prisoner must have passed it.'

In court Dr Jameson agreed that marks on the ploughshare were bloodstains. His view was that it had been used to strike down Steed 'before the boot went to work'. It was the share that had first shattered the skull. After that had come the kicking and stamping.

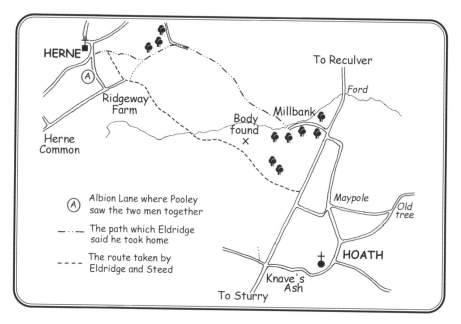

Murder site map.

As for the motive, that was clear. In February 1863 Steed had lent Eldridge some money. It is not known exactly what the sum was but it was doubtless no more than a matter of shillings. But when the debt was not repaid, trifling though it appears to have been, Steed had taken out a County Court summons against Eldridge. It must have seemed grossly unfair that a man who was running his own business should act so unreasonably towards a poor labourer. And it is incontestable that Eldridge did call at Steed's house one suppertime to make an attempt to pay off part of what he owed. He offered Steed a shilling but the coin was refused. It was now in the hands of the court, Steed said. There were high words exchanged and apparently Steed pushed Eldridge out of the house. 'Oh, you bugger,' Eldridge said, 'I'll do for you before many weeks.' On another occasion Eldridge called at the house and gave a shilling to one of Steed's young daughters, asking her to give it to her father but the money was sent back. One wonders if the matter might not have been resolved differently.

Alfred Eldridge appeared before Mr Justice Channell at the Maidstone Assizes on 3rd July 1863. There was little to add to what had been heard at the inquest and the magistrates' court. The stained clothing, the muddy boots with not only hair but red fibres from Steed's scarf, the witnesses who had seen Eldridge in the Prince Albert and those who had seen him outside with Steed, all made their appearance. Two warders who had brought Eldridge up from Canterbury to Maidstone said that on the way they heard him admit to the murder when talking to other prisoners. He had said, according to these witnesses, that he kicked out Steed's brains because of a disagreement over money and that he had been drunk at the time. Until the Sunday morning, he had told his fellow prisoners, he had not known that he was dead.

Eldridge's defence counsel had little on which to build a case. There was an attempt to plead that the evidence was simply circumstantial, but in fact much decisive evidence in cases both past and modern is circumstantial. There was motive (the debt), there was opportunity (the men were seen together), there was forensic detail (the stained trousers, the ploughshare) and there was the threat 'to do for' Steed.

After only fifteen minutes' deliberation, the jury returned with a guilty verdict and Eldridge was sentenced to hang.

In the condemned cell Eldridge confessed to murdering Steed but he did claim that he had been greatly provoked. He had met Steed at the Prince Albert on the Saturday evening and there had been no animosity between them. They had a drink together and then decided to walk home together. Witnesses stated that in the pub and as they went together homewards they appeared to be very amiable. But somewhere along the way the talk had turned to the debt and heated words had been exchanged. Steed, the condemned man said, had pushed him and he had warned him to stop. If he did not stop, Eldridge had told Steed, he would 'serve him out'. But Steed had pushed him again and Eldridge had knocked him to the ground. Then, enraged, he had stamped on him and kicked him although he said he had not intended to kill him. No mention was made of the ploughshare.

In the days before his execution Eldridge said that he felt happier than at any time since his boyhood. Perhaps the confession lifted a burden from a troubled conscience. On the Monday before he went to the scaffold his photograph was taken to send to his wife. Sadly he was unable to see her as she was ill, but she had written several affectionate letters to him.

Eldridge was executed along with another prisoner at the front of Maidstone prison on 20th August 1863. On the scaffold, Eldridge

*A public execution at Maidstone gaol. This was the cover of
a pamphlet describing the murder, trial and execution.*

looked around and is alleged to have said, 'I don't know why it is but I've never so happy in all my life.' And he added, 'Tell my wife that I am very happy and that I have no fear.' The white linen caps were placed over the condemned men's heads and then after they had shaken hands with the hangman, the trapdoor opened …

The *Kentish Gazette* reported: 'There were about 6,000 or 7,000 persons present, most of the very lowest orders, but the usual opportunity of gratifying their morbid tastes was denied them as the scaffold was so surrounded with black cloth that not more than the top of each white cap could be seen after the drop had fallen.'

That the murder was savage, that it was cruel, is undeniable. There is no doubt that Alfred Eldridge was guilty of a most brutal crime. But need matters have turned out this way? Without taking away any element of responsibility from Eldridge, might the deeply wronged Richard Steed have handled his dispute more wisely? Difficult to say, of course, after so long and with such limited resources. It's just a thought.

6

THE WICKED STEPMOTHER

Sometime after 10.30 pm on Sunday, 25th August 1867, the body of Louisa Kidder Staples, 11 years old, was recovered from the ditch in which she had drowned about quarter of a mile from New Romney. People had been out looking for her since eight o'clock and the local constable, Benjamin Aspinall, had been summoned and even before the body was retrieved, he had someone under arrest. It was Frances Kidder, the girl's stepmother. She was to face trial at Maidstone Assizes in March 1868. Kidder was ultimately sentenced to death, the last woman in the United Kingdom to be hanged in public.

In the course of the inquest, the hearings in the magistrates' court and the trial, there unfolded a tale of a woman who had frequently threatened to murder her stepchild and who eventually was as good as her word. Perhaps the most painful feature of the whole affair, the details of the girl's death apart, was the fact that even Frances Kidder's parents and her two sisters felt obliged to offer evidence against her.

Frances Turner of New Romney was 23 when in early 1865 she married William Kidder of Hythe, described variously as a greengrocer, potato salesman and general dealer. There had been a distinct reluctance on Kidder's part to commit himself to marriage even during Frances's pregnancy but after she had given birth to Emma and had then taken him before the magistrates at New Romney on a Summons of Affiliation, he had consented to marriage rather than face public exposure. It seems that Kidder was not in favour of marriage. A long relationship with a Miss (or possibly Mrs) Staples had ended with her death only a few months before. All save one of their union were old enough to look after themselves so that to his marriage to Frances Kidder he brought only one child, Louisa, who bore the surname Staples.

It was not a successful marriage. Too little is known about William Kidder to say the degree to which he was responsible for this. But what does seem certain is that as the parent of Louisa he was criminally neglectful. In none of the contemporary reports of this dramatic case is he ever criticised for failing to intervene in the abuse of his daughter. Other witnesses come forward with accounts of how the child was treated but nothing was ever done about it by William Kidder. He is like Cinderella's father. That tale is full of how wicked the stepmother is; never does he step in to take his much put-upon daughter away from the kitchen and off to the ball. She's lucky, a fairy godmother comes along. Then there's the Grimm tale *The Juniper Tree*, where the stepmother cuts off the child's head. And, again, where is the protective father? Missing. Just as he is in other folk and fairy tales. And the same here, in the real life case of Louisa Kidder Staples. Where is he? He remains a quite shadowy figure. Perhaps not directly guilty but too lax to save his daughter from daily harm and from living in constant anxiety.

Louisa's was a life of perpetual fear, which lasted a full two years from the time of her father's marriage in 1865 until her death. Listen to the testimony of the witnesses at the inquest, at the magistrates' court, at the Assizes. It is as plain as anything what was happening to the child. Witnesses told how Frances treated her stepdaughter with brutality, regularly. She had been seen thrashing Louisa with sticks while the girl screamed with agony. Sometimes neighbours had sheltered and fed her.

Corporal Isaac Sage was married to the sister of Louisa's real mother. He had known the child from infancy and he knew her father and stepmother intimately. 'I frequently saw the deceased,' he told the coroner's court. 'From the statements of the child to me she has been very badly used by her mother in law [sic]. I have frequently seen her with black eyes and bruises on her body, which she said had been given her by her stepmother, Mrs Kidder. Mrs Kidder was summoned to the court at Hythe on one occasion for ill-treating the child. She was punished by the magistrates, the authorities of the town prosecuted. The child's grandfather, who lives at Sellindge, several times came down to Hythe about the ill treatment of the child. On one occasion the child was taken away from Mrs Kidder by the police authorities at Hythe, on account of her cruel treatment and put out to keep, the father, I believe, having to pay for it ... I always feared Mrs Kidder would make away with the child. Louisa was small and rather cross-eyed. At one time she was a very lively, sprightly child but lately she has been quite dull and seemed to have no life in her. For the last two years she has been growing so, I have no doubt through the ill-usage to which she has been subjected.'

About seven weeks before Louisa's death, Frances had suffered an accident. Her husband's pony had run away out of control and she had been thrown out of the cart and dragged for fifty yards or so. Kidder was to refer to this accident later: 'When she came home she was in a fit for four hours,' he said, 'and she has been strange in her head ever since.' Mrs Maggie Burwell nursed Frances for four weeks, time enough to assess how Louisa was being treated by her stepmother. On one occasion she saw Frances push Louisa so that her head was hit against a table. The blow raised a lump as big as an egg. Another day Mrs Burwell heard her being beaten and later when she came downstairs, her apron was covered with blood. Yet another time Louisa came to Mrs Burwell screaming and again bleeding from the blows she had received. Sometimes the child was kept without food. When Mrs Burwell remonstrated with Frances she replied that she had a right to do what she liked with her child. During her month's stay, on one occasion Mrs Burwell heard Frances threaten Louisa with poison and another time she overheard her tell William that if he did not take the child away she would murder her. Even so, Mrs Burwell was to claim that she believed these were no more than empty threats made in anger.

At the Assizes, William Heaniker, who lived in a house adjoining the Kidders' said that he could hear all that passed next door. He said that he repeatedly heard Louisa being beaten. She was very much bruised and he recalled Frances being called up before the magistrates, though this, he said, had little effect. There had been one incident while her father was away when Louisa was thrown out into the street and Heaniker had taken her in. What is surprising about the statement of this witness is that he suggested that William Kidder was unaware of the constant cruelty to Louisa. Heaniker said the ill treatment generally occurred when Kidder was out of the house. This takes some believing. Can William Kidder have been so totally unaware of what was apparent to his neighbours? Heaniker further claimed to have heard Frances threaten Louisa, saying that she would break her neck if she dared to tell her father anything about her treatment.

In the last week of Louisa's life, Frances took her and baby Emma to her parents' home at New Romney. She said that her husband never liked her to go to her parents, although the reason for this is unclear. Certainly they come across, the father and mother and two sisters, as straightforward and honest. They would make no attempts to cover up what happened.

On Saturday, 17th August, Frances and the two children set off from Hythe and walked the nine or so miles to New Romney. Why William Kidder did not take them in the trap is not indicated but at that time people tackled much more strenuous walks then than is the practice today, so perhaps there was nothing extraordinary in the journey to New Romney. Nevertheless, one might wonder why it was that they set off in the evening, though that has no bearing on the murder. In her testimony, however, Frances stresses that it was dark nearly all the way and that it was almost 11 pm when they arrived at New Romney. It may be that she was trying to show that she had every opportunity to do away with Louisa on that journey had she been so minded.

At her parents' home the frightening threats and the physical violence continued. Frances's sister, Mary Turner, was witness to several threats to drown Louisa. Unlike Mrs Burwell, Mary did not believe they were just empty remarks made in anger. She had heard Frances tell Louisa quite calmly what was to be her fate, even when the girl was doing nothing wrong. And during that last week, Frances had quite openly told Mary that she did not intend to take Louisa back to Hythe. But why did Mary do nothing about these threats? Perhaps she could not really bring herself to believe that her sister was capable of such an act?

A local girl, 15-year-old Jane Smith, said that on the afternoon of Thursday, 22nd August she met Louisa, who showed her bruises on her neck. The previous night, she said, her stepmother had tried to strangle her and had warned her that she meant to make away with her before she went back to Hythe. She had threatened, Louisa said, to drown her in a ditch.

On the Saturday afternoon, Frances visited Eliza Evans, one of her parents' neighbours. Mrs Evans asked her about the child who had come with her. Was it Kidder's child, she had asked? 'Yes, a damned bastard,' was the reply, 'and I mean to get rid of her before I get home. I hate the very sight of her.' After that she had said that she hated other people's bastards.

Mrs Evans asked her why she hated the child. The answer was: 'Oh, because she is always making mischief and there will never be no peace all the time she is alive. Them you want to get rid of generally live the longest.' Astounded, Mrs Evans asked her what her husband thought. And this brings us back to Kidder and the doubts about him that persist. 'She said that her husband hated her as much as she did and would like to get rid of her as much.'

But give Frances an opportunity to have her say. Here she is at the magistrates' court, pleading her innocence and taking a chance to point a finger at her husband. 'I have always done my best for them all,' she says. 'He [Kidder] always said if he got half a chance he would serve me out and tell any lie against me. He once ill-used me very much and locked me out of doors. I had him up for it and he has been against me ever since. His child has been with me two years. I did my best for her in getting her clothes and keeping her clean and sending her to school. I could not do as I would have done because I had not the means. He would not let me have a farthing. The clothes I have I had before I had him.'

So it was an unhappy marriage, that much is evident. But was she offering that as the reason for her offence? She cannot blame Kidder for the murder of his daughter. There might be truth in his not caring much for the child but he was certainly not her murderer.

She goes on, 'I have always kept myself respectable before I was married … I never did anyone any harm nor yet wished them any. I have endeavoured to do my best by everyone and if I could help my friends I have always done so. I have not been out during my stay at New Romney till Sunday night last when I went out to meet my mother and father. I never cared to go out here. I wanted to get home again and I was expecting my husband down. That is why I stayed so long before I went out that evening.'

John Turner, her father, said that throughout the week of her stay his daughter 'had been low-spirited and on several occasions she had not taken her meals.' He was aware that she had attacked Louisa once, leaving purple marks on her neck. Again, there is no evidence of any positive attempt to save Louisa from her brutal treatment.

Doubtless the ineffective Turner family were relieved when the week's stay was nearly over. With a daughter obviously neurotic – though they would not have understood the term they would have recognised the condition – they must have suffered from her constant bouts of temper and tantrums. Kidder was due to come with the trap on the Sunday evening to collect his wife and children.

Just after 7 pm, Mr and Mrs Turner decided to go for an evening stroll and invited Frances to go out with them. She pleaded not feeling well and they left the house. Frances was left alone in the house with her youngest sister, 12-year-old Rhoda, baby Emma and Louisa. Was there no concern, no anxiety on the part of the parents about what might happen?

Frances told Rhoda that she might, if she wished, go out for a walk. After all it was still light. Would she like to take Emma with her? Of course she would. She would love to take the baby. Any child would delight in taking out her baby niece. But, Rhoda asked, could Louisa come as well. No, Frances replied, no, Louisa must stay at home. And so while Rhoda and Emma went off for their walk, Frances told Louisa, for no apparent reason to change out of her best frock. She probably told her that she had changed her mind that she would go for a walk, down through the fields to meet her parents. And Louisa would come with her.

Did any flickering suspicion enter the child's mind, any fear, any thought of what might happen? She knew her stepmother's uncertain and violent disposition. She had heard the threats of what would happen to her. Did that little 11-year-old girl have some foreboding as she left the house for the last time?

At about 8 pm the Turners came home from their stroll and found the house empty. They were instantly concerned about Louisa's welfare. They had heard their daughter's threats. The thought of her leading Louisa away at night into an area full of ditches, though they were generally shallow and stagnant, caused the parents deep anxiety. They left the house once more to search the neighbouring lanes and fields. They returned home again. Now Rhoda had come back with Emma but she was unable to shed any light on events. Her father went out yet again to continue his search and on his next return to the house found that William Kidder had turned up in the trap. It was now about 9.30 pm and it was dark. The two men went across the fields in different directions, both of them calling out the names of the missing woman and child.

At about 10 pm Frances arrived at the back door. She was alone. She beckoned to her mother and told her she was 'all wet'. She was bedraggled, the skirt of her dress soaked and muddy, as were the sleeves. But where was the child? There was no reply to the question and Mrs Turner called out the girl's name into the darkness behind. There was no answering call. None was expected. 'Where's the child?' Mrs Turner asked again. Her daughter did not answer but when the question was repeated, she nodded in the direction of the fields and ditches beyond, muttering 'Out there.'

'You haven't made away with the child?'

'Oh no, mother,' her daughter told her. 'But as we were coming home, two horses frightened us into a ditch. I went in after her and tried to get her out.'

At this point William Kidder joined the two women. Where was his daughter, he asked? 'I don't want to see you,' Frances replied. She went up to the bedroom and continued refusing to tell him where Louisa might be found. As she sat silent and sullen, Kidder indicated the skirts of her dress. 'I can see what you have been doing,' he told her and now, desperate no doubt, he summoned the local constable, Benjamin Aspinall. At the inquest, Kidder described what happened next.

'When he [the policeman] arrived he went upstairs for my wife and took her into custody. After my wife was taken into custody I went with Turner, the policeman, and others to the ditches and after searching for about 20 minutes found the deceased in a ditch. We got her out of the water but she was quite dead.'

Before the magistrates, Frances told the same story she had told her mother. She and Louisa had gone halfway to the seaside, she said, and had then turned and come back again. They got halfway across Mr Cobb's bridge and suddenly two rampaging horses came racing towards them. The child, frightened, had run along the bank and had fallen in the water. She had gone in to try to save her. She had screamed for help but no one had come. Then, when she had got out of the ditch, she ran home as fast as she could and told her mother what had happened. But she did not explain why it was that she had refused to answer any questions about Louisa's whereabouts.

On 12th March 1868 Frances Kidder appeared before Mr Justice Byles at the Spring Assizes at Maidstone, charged with the murder of her stepdaughter. There had been a long wait for her case to come to trial, as that year there had been no Winter Assizes. The Crown was represented by Mr Biron and Mr Dering but only at the last minute was Mr Channell appointed as her defence counsel by the judge. Neither her husband nor any of her relatives had retained an attorney and counsel to take on the case. Frances had therefore no effective defence, for Mr Channell had no opportunity to consult with his client or to prepare his arguments. That he presented a competent defence with little preparation was commented upon by the judge at the conclusion of the trial. But even the finest advocate, with all of the time in the world to prepare, would have been hard-pressed to save Frances Kidder.

Maidstone gaol.

PC Aspinall told the court how, when he had made the arrest, Frances told him, 'You will find the child just above Mr Cobb's bridge, where she fell in.' She told him that there had been an accident.

The constable described finding Louisa's body in a ditch below the bridge and about quarter of a mile from the Turners' house. 'The deceased was lying on her back; her head was under the water but her knees were a little out. The legs were slightly bent. We got the body out and took it to the Ship Inn.' He referred to the fact that he had found Frances in the bedroom in dry clothing with her wet and muddy clothing under the bed. He produced the clothing for the court: a pair of boots, a light muslin dress, two dress petticoats, a muslin jacket, a pair of stockings and a pair of drawers. The dress was water-stained and muddied for 14 inches from the bottom hem and the sleeves had obviously been up to the elbows in water.

Other witnesses spoke of seeing a woman and a child in a dark, shabby dress that evening walking in the area as dusk fell. One said that they seemed to be confused as to which direction they ought to take, turning first to the left and then to the right. Another witness told of hearing a noise like a child crying in Mr Cobb's field.

The prosecution's theory was that Frances had pushed the child into the ditch and had forcibly held her down until she drowned. The sluggish water was scarcely more than a foot deep and its shallowness was strongly emphasised. If she had fallen into that depth of water, Mr Biron claimed, Louisa could easily have struggled out unaided. But, the prosecution went on to say, if it were the case that she had fallen into the deeper part of the ditch, Frances's dress would have been soaked up to her waist, whereas only the bottom part of her dress was wet. And surely, the prosecution continued, the sleeves of her dress would have been wet beyond the elbows.

The defence argument was that Louisa had fallen into water three feet deep and that her body had floated down to where it was found in the shallower part of the ditch. It was here that Frances had entered the water to save her stepdaughter, Mr Channell argued. Why not test the theory that Louisa had been forcibly held down, he proposed. Why not draw off the water in the ditches through the sluices and see if the mud revealed signs of a struggle? As for Frances's passionate expressions of temper, the defence counsel tried to convince the jury that these were often made in the heat of the moment by many people every day; they did not signify intent to murder. But Mr Channell's valiant rearguard fight was to no avail.

The summing up by Mr Justice Byles reviewed the arguments thoroughly and fairly. But, he asked, if there had been an accident, why had Frances not raised the alarm at once? Why, when asked, had she not responded to questions about Louisa's whereabouts? Why had she made statements so inconsistent and incredible? The prosecution arguments, the judge said, pointed all one way but if there was a single fact in the evidence inconsistent with guilt then the jury should acquit.

The jury retired for just twelve minutes and returned with a guilty verdict. Frances's execution was scheduled for 2nd April. In the condemned cell, perhaps unsurprisingly, she was reported to be sullen and morose. The Kent Messenger said that 'she appears to think she is ill-used by being placed in her present position but she has never denied her guilt.'

There might have been some faint hope of a reprieve for Frances when it was learnt that 'the mayor of Hythe and other gentlemen of that town are interesting themselves in her behalf and a petition will shortly be sent to the Home Office asking for a commutation of the sentence.' But it failed.

On execution day outside the main gate of Maidstone prison a crowd of 2,000, many of them women, turned out to witness what would be

Death certificate of Frances Kidder. (Crown Copyright. Reproduced with permission of the Controller of HMSO)

the last public execution of a woman in the United Kingdom. They gaped as Frances was helped up the steps to the gallows; they watched as her wrists were strapped in front and a leather belt was wrapped round her body and arms; they stared as, with a nod in the direction of female modesty, to prevent her skirt billowing up, a second belt was fastened round her legs. Then came prayer, the white cotton hood, and the creak of the bolt ...

Bad, then? Or mad? Both?

But what about those who heard all of the threats, who knew about the beatings? What about them? What about the neighbours, the friends? What about the husband, the father, the mother, the sisters? What about the Hythe magistrates? Were any of them partly responsible?

OBSESSION

It must be a nightmare – well, a worry – when the organist falls ill and is unable to come to Sunday service. What if no one else in the village can play the organ? What's the curate-in-charge to do? What if he hasn't a good enough voice to lead the hymns himself? That was precisely the problem faced by the Rev Mr Raven of Biddenden. Mr Bourne had sent his apologies on the Saturday. He was unwell, wouldn't be able to come the next day. He was sorry but ... then, almost out of the blue, there was a volunteer. It was Bertha Peterson. She'd do the morning and the evening services, she said. She'd need a bit of practice, of course. Couldn't just turn up and rattle off the music. But if Mr Bourne's daughter, May, would come along to the church early on the Sunday morning, just for a run-through on the harmonium, Miss Peterson would cope. Mr Raven was undoubtedly very relieved.

In a way, it was just chance that Miss Peterson was back in the village. She had turned up on the Wednesday and was staying at the Rose Inn, apparently until the Monday. More surprisingly, after morning service she was going to make a formal presentation of a picture in the infants' schoolroom. She'd brought it down from Reigate where she was then living. It was a fine engraving, beautifully mounted, and Mr Raven was sure that Christ, the Good Shepherd would be a real acquisition to the school.

In fact, as people observed, there had been something of a transformation as far as Miss Peterson was concerned. She was out and about in Biddenden, talking to people, very affable, most pleasant. Well, some people had never found her other than agreeable and ladylike when she'd lived in the village. Eccentric, yes, but then that's what a lot of these educated folk were often like. That's what many locals thought. After all, she was the rector's daughter and if a rector's daughter can't be a bit odd, then who could? Anyway, she used to do an awful lot of good in the parish.

Not that everybody would agree with that conclusion. For the rector's daughter to be seen walking down the village street in her dressing gown, and 'otherwise unsuitably apparelled', wasn't natural. It just wasn't normal. And furthermore, she had thrown her weight around from time to time. She had upset some people. Truth is that when she left the village a couple of years earlier, in 1897, there were those who could be excused for thinking 'Good riddance'.

For instance, Miss Thirkell, a church worker, had experienced a very unfortunate falling-out with Miss Peterson who had wished the Village Institute to be affiliated to the White Cross League, which helped children in need of protection. Miss Thirkell's resistance to the idea had led to much unpleasantness. They had not managed to make it up before Miss Peterson had gone off.

The ladylike Bertha Peterson,
Kentish Express.

Nor was it just with Miss Thirkell that Miss Peterson had had these upsets. She had also had been quite hostile in her dealings with the churchwardens, Mr Pinyon and Mr Lavence. The two men had always got on well with her father but eventually he had become too frail to bother much with church affairs and Miss Peterson seemed to think that she was in charge of the parish. In the end she used to ignore Mr Lavence as if he were of no account. Some thought it was perhaps because he was just a bus driver, but there were other real issues. For instance, that business with poor John Whibley, the Sunday school teacher, was really dreadful. Her differences with Whibley had begun as far back as February 1893 but in the early months of 1897 they reached a crucial point. When they did so, Mr Lavence had rejected Miss Peterson's demands, refusing to play any part in an investigation into what he called no more than hearsay. In his opinion it was absolutely wrong to start interrogating the chap on a seemingly baseless rumour. No matter, she'd managed to hound Whibley out of the Sunday school. She had even demanded that he stay away from Holy Communion. He couldn't stand up to her. She had her way and Whibley was out.

Nor did she give up her pursuit of Whibley. When asked for her usual annual contribution to the well-established charity, the Ancient Order of Foresters Friendly Society, she refused because Whibley was the secretary. The Gardeners' Society in the village was treated similarly, just because of Whibley's membership.

But now in February 1899 Bertha Peterson was back. And, what's more, all sweetness and light. She wanted to put the past behind her, wanted to express her regrets for what had happened. That is what she told people.

On the Friday she met Mr Lavence and they had what appeared to be a cordial meeting. She told him that she had come to the village for a specific purpose. 'I am going to make a public apology to those I offended in the parish,' she said. She mentioned the picture she was going to present. Would he come to the presentation after service on Sunday? Just a little affair, nothing elaborate, but she wished to acknowledge publicly how difficult she had been in the past. She spoke to Mr Pinyon and Miss Thirkell in similar vein.

John Whibley, the Sunday school teacher, Daily Graphic.

For John Whibley there was a personal letter, expressing the same kind of regrets. 'I would like to meet you in the school, shake hands and forgive and forget,' she had written. Would he come to the little ceremony? Of course he would. He was overjoyed. After all the hurtful innuendo of the past, Miss Peterson would retract all that she had said.

On the Sunday morning Miss Peterson went to church early to try out the hymns and chants for morning service with Miss Bourne.

Their practice went very well. Now what about rehearsing for this evening's service, Miss Bourne asked her. No, Miss Peterson replied. She would only become confused. For the time being she would just concentrate on the morning service.

Miss Peterson's playing at the service was very satisfactory. At Communion she had even knelt next to Whibley. Those who knew what had gone before might have thought it a symbolic moment in their relationship.

At the end of the service Miss Peterson made her way over to the infants' schoolroom, with its rows of hard, dark benches, its walls adorned with customary religious texts and a map of the Empire. She unwrapped the picture and placed it on top of the harmonium. Then in came the curate Mr Raven and Mr Whibley, the only ones who had responded to her invitation. The others, Miss Thirkell and the two churchwardens, had been deterred by illness and rain. Or so they said. It is difficult to believe that such significant church members would allow bad weather to keep them away from morning service. Had they really found that they could not accept Miss Peterson's apology? Had they been too deeply hurt in the past to feel able to shake hands?

But one old enemy was there. Whibley had gone over to a table to lay down his hat and walking stick. Miss Peterson went over to him. 'Oh, Mr Whibley,' she said, 'I wish to present a subscription to the Gardeners' Society.' She handed him an envelope containing two sovereigns. And then she said, 'Please look well at this picture.' Whibley went over to the harmonium where the beautifully engraved picture stood. It was then that Miss Peterson took a Colt revolver out of her pocket. She put it to Whibley's right ear and pulled the trigger.

And Mr Raven? He must have wondered if she was going to turn the weapon on him next. He did not wait but fled the schoolroom. Outside he met the schoolmaster, Mr Houghton, who lived at the schoolhouse. He had heard the shot and had come out of the house and met the curate who stammered out what had occurred. Houghton went towards the school building and met Miss Peterson at the entrance. She held the gun towards him. 'You can have this now,' she said. 'I had to do it to protect the children.' The schoolmaster was stunned. 'Miss Peterson,' he asked, 'whatever made you do this?' She made no reply, simply strolled past the astonished man into the High Street.

Only minutes later Houghton and another villager, Lacy Avery, a harness maker, caught up with Miss Peterson. She told them she wanted

The body in the schoolroom, as illustrated in the Kentish Express.

to go to the Rose Inn where she was staying. They had to persuade her to return with them to the school. She made no resistance but was at pains to point out that she had good reasons for what she had done. 'I suppose, Mr Avery, you know what I did this for,' she explained to him in reasonable tones. 'I suppose you know a woman is justified in killing a man but a child is not able. I did this to protect little children.'

Shortly afterwards Police Constable Mongham came on the scene. He examined the body, heard briefly what had occurred and then led Miss Peterson across the street to the Chequers Inn where, in a private room, the constable questioned her. But she had her own question for him. 'Where have you gentlemen been, to allow that man to outrage little children?'

Later at Cranbrook police station, when she was charged by Superintendent Thomas Fowle, although she seemed quite rational, she admitted without hesitation, 'I shot him.'

The search of her room at the Rose Inn revealed 43 rounds of .32 ammunition. The revolver handed to the schoolmaster, Mr Houghton, contained another five rounds. In the schoolroom were found more envelopes with money destined for local groups. One read: 'Enclosed one guinea subscription to day school, February 4th, 1899 B S Peterson'.

Murders do happen in places like Biddenden, though perhaps one feels that they ought not to do so. It is as if such a noble old community, with its traditions, its charities, its wonderful old timbered structures, possessing all the characteristics of a typical Kentish village, could have no truck with such immoderate acts. But here was Miss Bertha Peterson giving the lie to such expectations.

The *Kentish Express* can have had few such excitements and within hours it was covering the case with a meticulous attention to detail. The inquest was held on the Monday afternoon. 'When a representative of the *Kentish Express* visited the school on Monday morning he saw the body lying just as it fell. Underneath the head was a pool of blood, a ghastly spectacle indeed being presented … When seen by our representative the body was fully dressed but before the inspection by the jury some of the clothing was removed to admit of the post-mortem examination by the medical man.'

The newspaper was quick to assert in its first report that John Whibley was 'the victim of Miss Peterson's mania – for sane she surely cannot be.' Over the next few weeks and months as the case trailed its way to the Assizes, the full story was presented to an astonished public. It transpired that Miss Peterson's aged father was still officially Rector of Biddenden though quite unable to fulfil any role in the church. He was now living with relatives in Devon. One Sunday, two or three years earlier, he had been removed by relatives from the Rectory. He had been sorely neglected by his daughter, though not wilfully, certainly not with any intention of harming him. Nevertheless, he did observe that his daughter was 'as mad as a hatter'.

Miss Bertha Peterson, now 42 years old, was described in the newspaper as 'a woman of fine physique'. The reporter at the police court proceedings at Cranbrook on the Monday morning comments on her 'prepossessing appearance and notwithstanding the fact that she had passed the night in one of the little cells she entered the courtroom in a stately and unconcerned manner, apparently not the least affected by the gravity of the charge preferred against her.' He went on to describe her as tall and graceful in appearance, a woman of refined features. And he was possibly impressed by someone who had the panache to wear a pince-nez.

Since leaving Biddenden in 1897 Miss Peterson had rented Hillside, a cottage at Egerton, where she was regarded as 'a thoroughly nice lady'. She was only infrequently at Hillside, however, as she had taken up a post at Lady Henry Somerset's Industrial Farm Colony at Duxhurst near Reigate. Here, at what was a home for inebriates, she had charge of one of the houses for inmates.

But all the time she was at Duxhurst she was brooding. Something preyed on her mind. She frequently talked about it to the matron and doubtless to any others who would listen. It was John Whibley. She was obsessed with the man whom she believed had committed an indecent assault on a member of his Sunday school class.

Whatever the root of her obsession, Bertha Peterson would constantly assert that her motive in killing him was to rid the world of a child abuser. Two years earlier, she had sent him a letter. It read:

The Rectory, 16th March 1897

Mr Whibley, I have learnt that you are generally thought to have committed an atrocious crime against God and against an innocent, defenceless member of Christ – a little girl. I will not tell you how I learnt this. It is not necessary to do so, seeing that everyone to whom I have applied for evidence to clear you is not only unable to give any such evidence, but refers me to several more people who are also unable to help my researches in your defence. You are a communicant and a Sunday school teacher and I ask you, in God's name, two questions:

1. Are you innocent of this crime?
2. Can you tell me how I can clear you?

I will spare neither time, thought, nor money, and no exertion shall be too great for me if you will tell me how to do it. I await your answer.

Bertha S.H. Peterson.

But she had no doubt that she could not clear him. To her, he was guilty. Nor was this the first letter. On several previous occasions she had

The house where Whibley lived in Biddenden, Kentish Express.

written in a very disagreeable fashion to Whibley and his wife. Today, of course, the recipient of such a letter would go straight to a solicitor. But over 100 years ago it was less easy. It was too expensive. And who would believe a shoemaker accused by a rector's daughter, a well-educated woman, a woman from a highly respectable family, a woman who rode to hounds? No matter how highly regarded he was in Biddenden, how would he have fared in a court of law?

Though he did not face a court of law, Whibley was summoned to the Rectory where he underwent an inquisition, questioned, accused, by Miss Peterson and her close friend, Miss Gould, a younger woman who completely accepted her mentor's position on the matter of Whibley. He denied the charge, saying he would take his solemn oath that he was innocent. That was not enough for Miss Peterson. Dissatisfied with his response, she wrote to the Archbishop of Canterbury, the Rural Dean and the churchwardens, appealing to them to take action in order to protect children from him. In a letter to a Miss

Oliver in Canterbury she wrote that 'the fate of Sodom and Gomorrah' was hanging over Biddenden.

At the various hearings at the magistrates' court and at the Assizes, Miss Peterson's visit to the Army and Navy Stores in London was described. She had gone there to buy her revolver. Then a fortnight before the shooting she had visited her cottage at Egerton for the weekend. She had attached a five-inch square of wood from a Tate sugar box to a tree and used it as a target. When it was presented in court the target bore the marks of fifty cartridges. The powder marks suggested that she had fired from very close range, almost with the muzzle touching the wood.

Despite all, when she appeared in court, Bertha Peterson was always assured and unruffled. On the day of her trial at Maidstone Assizes before Mr Justice Matthew she seemed little concerned. She had breakfasted well in the gaol on filleted plaice and toast and her other meals, always provided from outside the prison, were certainly better than those offered to other inmates.

In the course of the trial a number of Miss Peterson's personal letters to her friend Alice Gould were read out. The intention was to portray the depth of her conviction that John Whibley had committed 'an atrocious crime'. At the inquest the coroner had expressed his view that she regarded herself in the light of a Divine Avenger, and the letters quite clearly show that she believed she was fulfilling God's purpose.

Before commenting further on what was in the letters, it may be appropriate to say something about Alice Gould and her relationship with Bertha Peterson. They had first met in 1883 when Alice was only 11 years old and Miss Peterson 26. In May 1895 Alice had gone to live with Miss Peterson and her father at the Rectory. In November 1897 they had left Biddenden and had gone to Egerton. They had then separated in May 1898 when Miss Peterson went to work in the home at Duxhurst. But they had not lost contact and they retained their deep affection for each other.

How this relationship was viewed in late Victorian Kent is impossible to say. There must have been raised eyebrows. But perhaps, despite the wording of some of the letters, the relationship was no more than that of a caring woman for a younger friend. The most important reason for the letters being produced was to illustrate Miss Peterson's state of mind, which Alice Gould admitted would 'magnify small things and minimise big things', especially where these concerned the welfare of small girls. Miss Peterson, she said, had been distressed about the story concerning John Whibley and a girl in the parish and she had believed that the shoemaker had paid someone to hush up the matter.

The letters read out by the prosecution reveal a woman obsessed, convinced that she was acting in accordance with Divine Will. A letter dated 6th February reads: 'My own darling little one, God told me to do it and told me to do what I have done. I shot the man JW. If you knew how I felt, dear, it would help me to bear it. I am quite happy except for you. ...I love you, my lamb.'

Another letter, written to Miss Gould, for no obvious reason in French, repeats her conviction: 'God is with you, have no fear. God told me to do it, therefore it is right ... If our hearts are broken and we have to go through agonies we shall have helped to save little girls.'

A third of several letters concludes: 'God told me that I should be pardoned.'

It was all too easy for the jury to believe Dr Davies, the Medical Superintendent of the asylum at Barming Heath, who had come to the conclusion that the prisoner was suffering from delusions. She refused to accept the shooting as a crime, claiming that she was fulfilling God's command.

Dr Hele Bate who had known Miss Peterson for eight years said that she was very excitable and, at times, extremely eccentric. 'I cannot say I thought she was insane,' he told the court, 'but she was bordering on it. Her extreme eccentricity was bordering on insanity.'

How the trial would conclude must have been obvious from the start. As it turned out, Mr Justice Matthew ordered Miss Peterson to be detained during Her Majesty's pleasure. She was sent to an asylum where she spent over fifty years, dying in the early 1950s, never expressing remorse for her crime. Bertha Peterson, that most unfortunate of women, who was both affectionate and kind-hearted, was dangerously deluded.

Whether there were grounds for her accusation against John Whibley is not known. Another matter – which mercifully was not resolved – was what would have happened to her old adversaries, Mr Lavence and Mr Pinyon and Miss Thirkell, had they turned up as invited in the infant schoolroom. Had she plans for them too? After all there were still bullets in the chamber of the revolver when she handed it over to the schoolmaster.

PRINTS

This is an account of a grubby, vicious crime carried out by two low-level criminals. It would have been long forgotten, taking its place alongside hundreds of similarly undistinguished murders, had it not been that this was the first murder trial to feature fingerprint evidence. The Stratton brothers, Alfred aged 22 and Albert, 20, take their place in crime's long corridor of infamy solely because of this single fact. Their trial in 1905 was a landmark in the history of forensic evidence. At last it became acceptable to use fingerprints to break down the alibis of murderers and to prove their guilt.

The three-man fingerprint bureau was established at Scotland Yard in 1901 by the Commissioner, Sir Edward Henry, who was enthusiastic for the adoption of fingerprinting as a means of identifying criminals. Since 1870 records of criminals had frequently borne photographs and notes on the height of criminals, the width of their head, the size of their ears, the length of their arms and legs. But it was a totally unreliable method and increasingly, after the arrival of Sir Edward at Scotland Yard, convicted criminals had their prints taken and filed in the bureau's records. As a result Sir Edward and his Assistant Commissioner, Sir Melville McNaughton, had more and more successes in the courts with fingerprinting evidence in non-capital crimes. Even so, some judges had strong reservations about such innovation. It was the so-called 'Mask Murders Case' in which Alfred and Albert Stratton were brought to justice that really promoted the legitimacy of this new method of identifying criminals. Perhaps the brothers might have had some faint awareness of the significance of their case and how it had been resolved by the police but that was to be of little consolation to them.

But now to turn-of-the-century Deptford, rough, violent, impoverished, with little to raise the spirit in its squalid streets, its jerrybuilt terraces, its shabby shops. Life here was a struggle, often unrewarded, without hope for many, no matter how they tried. Even its criminals seemed to lack ambition, battening as they did for the most part on those as poor as they were. In this squabbling, brawling, raging world there was little protection for the vulnerable. And it was here that the brothers grew up, pursuing their modest goals with a reckless violence that took no heed of anyone else.

It would be incorrect to imagine that Deptford, despite its reputation, was occupied exclusively by criminals. As always the majority of people were law abiding, going about their work conscientiously at the docks and factories, the shops and markets. For instance, take the Farrows, a hard working, respectable, decent couple. For more than 50 years Thomas Farrow had managed George Chapman's chandlery selling candles, varnish, oil, rope, soap, paint and paraffin at 34 High Street. For the greater part of that time his wife, Ann, had worked with him in the shop but more recently he had taken on a boy, William Jones, in her place.

Farrow opened up The Oil and Colour Store each morning at eight o'clock and did not close until 9.30 pm. Every Monday morning the shop's owner, George Chapman, called to collect the previous week's takings. Farrow would hand over the cash – usually something in the order of £12 (a large sum in those days) in a paper parcel quite unostentatiously. The whole of the previous week's takings were always in the shop premises on Sunday nights.

The old couple customarily went to bed at about 10.30 pm and they probably did so on the night of Sunday, 26th March. But on the next morning the shop was not opened at the usual eight o'clock. When Jones, the shop lad, arrived for work at 8.30 am, the doors were still firmly locked. Puzzled by this turn of events, he tried the door at the rear but it too was locked, nor did all his hammering and shouting back and front rouse anyone inside. Finally he enlisted the help of Louis Kidman, the manager of another of George Chapman's nearby shops, and together the two climbed through a window at the rear.

The building was silent, both the living quarters and the shop area at the front. There was no response to their anxious calls. And then they found a body. In the middle of the living room floor was the old man, his head battered in, his face a mask of blood. And upstairs in the bedroom where furniture had been thrown about, where cupboards had been turned out and drawers emptied, where there was a scene of total disorder, lay old Ann Farrow, stretched out across the bed, her head also severely beaten. She was still alive though unconscious.

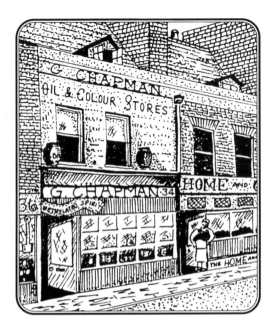

The shop in Deptford where the Farrows worked.

The police were sent for and Sergeant Atkinson was first on the scene. He questioned Jones and Kidman and waited for the arrival of the ambulance men. He spotted a metal cashbox on the floor. Clearly it had been forced open. That was important. The sergeant reached down and pushed in under the bed. He did not wish it to be trampled on by the ambulance men when they came for Ann Farrow.

Then Detective Inspector Hailstone from Deptford police station arrived at the house and later Chief Inspector Frederick Fox from Scotland Yard joined him to take charge of the investigation. They inspected the cashbox and found a smudged fingerprint on the varnished inner tray. Assistant Commissioner McNaughton was sent for. It was just the kind of case for which he had been waiting. Now arrangements were made for the cashbox to be taken, carefully wrapped in paper, to the fingerprint bureau. But Sergeant Atkinson had touched the cashbox. In his anxiety to preserve it from the feet of the ambulance men he had pushed it under the bed. He had never given thought to fingerprinting. After all it was not usual procedure. But he need not have worried. He was told to go the bureau and to have his fingerprints taken so that they could be eliminated from the enquiry.

During the search of the building for clues police came across two black masks made out of stockings. So, the police were looking for two men. Why were they wearing masks? Might this suggest that they were local men, possibly recognisable to the victims? And had they brought the masks with them? Had they come prepared? That seems likely because later the police were to discover similar masks among the

Prints

property of the Strattons. Though it is not especially important it may be worth knowing that the police thought that the brothers had fashioned the masks out of Ann Farrow's stockings, which they had found on the ground floor. It might serve, of course, to demonstrate how hopelessly disorganised the Strattons were as thieves if they suddenly decided to make masks for themselves mid-job.

What had happened was not difficult for the police to work out. The men had gained entry at the rear of the house, perhaps in the early hours of the morning. That they should break in on Sunday when a week's takings were on the premises was another indication that these were men with local knowledge. They had searched downstairs, presumably for the cashbox, and had made enough noise to rouse Thomas Farrow. He had groped his way down the gas-lit stairway and was confronted by the intruders. They had wasted no time threatening him. They hadn't bothered to force him to tell them where the money was kept. Had the old man done so, surely they would have left him and his wife unharmed. But it seems that he was attacked almost straightaway. Some have suggested that it was panic that forced such a violent reaction. Others, more convincingly, have said that the thieves acted as such people always react, with total thoughtless violence. Why should the old man come down and get in the way? How dare he? And so they set about him with some blunt instrument, a crowbar or a cosh, some weapon that would crack his skull that would shut him up for ever. It is the way of the thug.

And then upstairs they go to where Ann calls out timorously to her husband. She has heard the cries, the thuds downstairs. She knows something dreadful has happened. Then she hears the tread of a man, of two men, coming up the stairs. And they burst in the room, these two masked figures. They face the old woman in the dark. Like her husband, dead downstairs, she is an obstacle, a nuisance. She is in the way, just as her husband was. And she is attacked ...

And after they have turned the room upside down, after they have discovered the cashbox and have prised it open, they leave by the front door. Havoc leaves the house.

Ann Farrow was taken to hospital but she never regained consciousness. Now the police had a double murder to solve. The newspapers billed it as the 'Mask Murders Case'. But at the Yard they might have thought of it as the 'Fingerprint Murders Case', the first of its kind.

A massive police operation was mounted. When the fingerprints of the Farrows were taken – the first occasion on which fingerprints were taken from corpses – it was established that the print on the tray of the cashbox did not come from either of them, but neither was it from any in the collection of tens of thousands of prints already held in police records. Hundreds of people in Deptford, honest and otherwise, were interviewed. A milkman said that shortly before seven o'clock on the morning of the murder he had seen a couple of men leaving the shop. And Ethel Stanton who had been in the High Street at the crucial time talked of seeing two men, young, shabbily dressed. One of them wore brown boots and a brown overcoat. They had left the shop by the front door. They had started running as soon as they closed the door behind them. But neither witness could remember much else about the men.

Deptford was not the easiest place for police enquiries. Even so, there was some feeling even among the criminal fraternity (in fact, it is nothing like a fraternity when things go wrong!) that this crime was excessive, something that they could not sympathise with. The murder of an old couple was quite beyond the understanding of even the most hardened criminals. And there was some talk about the Stratton brothers, which made its way to the two local policemen, Detective Inspector Hailstone and Detective Sergeant Gall. Although there was no fingerprint record of either brother, the policemen certainly wished to speak to them But Alfred and Albert were nowhere to be found.

Well, what about their friends, their acquaintances? Were there girl friends? Were they running prostitutes, as seems likely? Detective Sergeant Gall found one of Alfred's girls, Helen Cromarty, living in Brookmill Road. She was sporting a black eye. Alfred had called on her on the Monday morning, she said, and had lain down and gone to sleep. Being short of money, she had taken the opportunity to rifle his pockets. She'd found a heavily bloodstained handkerchief. Unfortunately for her, Alfred had wakened and had punched her. And where was he now, she was asked. But all of the detective's assurances that she would be looked after if she let on where Alfred was now staying were useless. She wouldn't say. Tell on Alfred? He'd kill her. She daren't. But she changed her mind very quickly when she was told that she would be arrested as an accessory to murder. Brockwell Street, she told him. Brockwell Street in Stratford. They'd find him there.

Under questioning, she told Chief Inspector Fox and Gall that she had, in fact, been at home with Alfred when the brothers went off to do the job. The one in the High Street, she said. Sometime early on the Monday morning, Albert had come to her ground floor lodgings and had knocked on the window. He'd asked Alfred if he was ready and the two of them had gone off. She knew they were off to burgle some place but she had no idea of the details.

Later in the morning Alfred had returned at about nine o'clock. He said that he had been to the public baths to clean up. Then he told the girl that she was his alibi. If the police asked where he was in the early hours of Monday she was to tell them that he'd spent the whole night with her. They'd gone to bed early and stayed there. She hadn't suspected that they had committed a murder, she said. Her thoughts were that they'd just gone out on an ordinary job.

After having breakfast Alfred had blacked his boots and it was after that, when he had fallen asleep, that she had gone through his pockets and he had punched her.

Then he had gone out, wearing his brown coat. When he came back his coat was missing. He told her he was moving out, going to Stratford. Just for a while. He was going to Brockwell Street. And no, she hadn't had anything to do with any burglary. She just knew that that was why they had gone out. It was only when she had heard about the murder that she suspected that the brothers must have been involved. And she had no idea where Albert had gone.

The search for the brothers intensified. But the police visit to the Brockwell Street address produced nothing. The bird had flown. It was known, though, that both brothers were keen Crystal Palace fans and there was a cup-tie there on the next Saturday. However, in spite of an intense plain-clothes presence at the match, there was no sign of either man.

But then there came another whisper. Some days later one of Alfred's so-called friends, questioned by police, was asked if had he seen Alfred. Alfred Stratton? Course, he had. He'd just left him in a pub in Evelyn Street. Easy. Hailstone went to the bar and arrested him. At Blackheath police station, before he was charged by Sergeant Beavis, Alfred, playing either the innocent or the smart Alec, asked why he was there. 'What for, Mr Beavis?' he asked. 'For poncing [pimping]?'

With Alfred in the cells and now fingerprinted, the search went on for Albert. A girl called Katie Wade revealed his current address, but when the police arrived Albert had gone, leaving behind him, in his haste, stolen clothing and silverware. He had also left three stocking

Alfred Stratton (left) and his brother Albert at trial, Daily Sketch.

masks similar to those found in the chandler's shop. Eventually Albert was run to earth in a Stepney lodging house.

The trial was held at the Old Bailey on 6th May before Mr Justice Channell. Without the print found on the cashbox, there might have been just enough evidence in this case to squeeze a guilty verdict. But Sir Edward Henry knew that this was the ideal opportunity to prove the worth of fingerprint evidence. The print matched exactly Alfred Stratton's right thumb. Sir Melville McNaughton, the Assistant Commissioner, wrote later: '... the circumstantial evidence gathered by Chief Inspector Fox and his associates before the trial was ... very strong and it is likely that the fingerprint was taken by the jury as confirmatory evidence. Inspector Charles Stockley Collins gave a little lecture on fingerprints from the witness box with the aid of a big chart and some impressions taken from the fingers of a jury man.'

In his 'little lecture' Collins explained that there were between 80,000 and 90,000 sets of fingerprints on file, which meant that there were 800,000 to 900,000 digits recorded. He explained that on examining

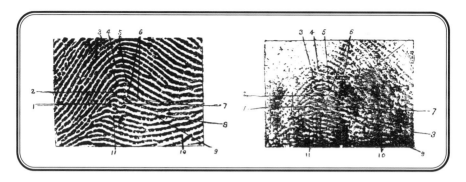

Right thumbprint (left) of Alfred Stratton, and thumbprint (right) found on the cashbox at 34 High Street, Deptford.

these impressions he had never found two separate ones to agree in their characteristics. The members of the jury were given magnifying glasses and copies of the fingerprints of the Strattons as well as copies of the print found on the cashbox. Collins took them through a whole new science of whorls, ridges, lakes and peninsulas, those individual characteristics of the human finger. He told them that fingerprints do not change. He showed that Alfred's right thumb bore eleven points of similarity to the mark on the cashbox.

In reply, the defence produced its own expert witness, Dr John Garson, who attempted to destroy the fingerprint evidence by stating that the measurement between certain points on the print were at variance. Indeed he was prepared to state on oath that the fingerprint on the cashbox was not identical with that of Alfred's right thumb. Prior to the trial Dr Garson had offered his expert services in writing to both to the prosecution and the defence. Perhaps this rather weakens our faith in his expertise, but, of course, the jury was unaware that he was willing to support whoever would pay him.

Mr Justice Channell revealed himself to be cautious about this new kind of evidence and the inferences to be drawn from it. During his summing up, he made his uncertainty about fingerprinting very obvious: 'If it is true that there are such differences as has been stated between people's finger marks, then there is an extraordinary resemblance between the photo of the finger marks on the japanned box and the photos of Alfred Stratton's fingers.' But he added for the record, 'Yet I am of the opinion that the jury would not like to act on this evidence alone. When proper impressions are taken, the system is extremely reliable. But it is a different thing to apply it to a casual mark made through the perspiration of a thumb.' He seemed to be implying that in future offenders should leave complete sets of fingerprints before they could be admitted as evidence.

The jury took two hours before returning a guilty verdict and it might be that some of them experienced the same kind of reservations as the judge. Future juries, however, would act on such evidence with less hesitation.

Three weeks after the trial the brothers, now blaming each other for what had happened, were hanged at Wandsworth. Vicious little third-rate criminals they were, but they will always be recalled by crime historians for the part they played in the history of fingerprinting.

THE BADGE AND BUTTON MURDER

On the cold and rainy midnight of Saturday, 9th February 1918, Mr Trew reported his 16-year-old daughter, Nellie, missing. She had left her home in Juno Terrace at Eltham Well to go to the library, and had not returned. It was unlike her. She regularly went to change her books on Saturday nights and was usually home by nine o'clock. Her parents had seen her at about seven o'clock when she left the house but now she was hours overdue. After all, Plumstead library was only a couple of miles or so away and she would go there and back by tram. She shouldn't be so late. Something must have happened to her. And no, Mr Trew reassured the constable on duty, she wasn't the sort of girl who stayed out all hours. She was very much the other way. And she hadn't a boyfriend. His wife and he had tried to find her, he said. They had gone out to see if there was any sign. They had waited by the tram stop. They had walked up by the park. They had done everything they could.

It was not until the next morning that Nellie Trew's body, a huddled shape, was found about 40 yards from the road on Eltham Common, opposite Shooters Hill cemetery. Police arrived and dispersed a crowd that had collected. She lay face upwards in what was described as 'a muddy swamp'. She was plastered with mud, top to toe, back and front, and had obviously put up a struggle against her attacker. Her face was heavily bruised and bloodied from a blow to the mouth and there were bruises on each side of the windpipe. Nellie Trew, a school leaver only six months earlier, an attractive, lively girl, had been raped and strangled with considerable force. Her body lay less than a quarter of a mile from her home, only yards from where, only hours earlier, her anxious parents had searched for her, calling her name in vain.

Scattered around about 40 yards from the body and nearer to the roadway were some of her possessions: a hair slide and hat pin, a

Nellie Trew.

threepenny piece, her library book – *Adventures of her Baby* – and a handbag. It seemed clear that the struggle had begun about six yards from the pavement and then Nellie either had fled or was carried further onto the common. She had put up a ferocious struggle, her high-heeled shoes ploughing up the ground. But finally she had been left dead or dying in the dark, damp February night. Only her hat, still secured to her head by one hatpin, had withstood the struggle.

The open ground had been so cut up by the sightseers that it was impossible to identify the murderer's footprints from those whose curiosity had led them to the spot.

Nellie had lost a considerable amount of blood from the blow to the face and her other injuries. The murderer's clothes would be deeply stained. And there were two possible clues. Trodden into the ground was a button from an overcoat and a replica of a soldier's cap badge.

Apart from these two items the police had little to go on. The badge showed a tiger with a swishing tail and a raised right paw, the emblem of the Leicestershire Regiment. It was only a copy, however, not an authentic badge as worn by soldiers, and unlikely therefore to belong to a serving soldier. The overcoat button was unique in that a piece of wire was threaded through its holes. Odd, that. Wire, not cotton thread. But there was nothing to say that it, any more than the badge, had come from the murderer's coat.

Sir Bernard Spilsbury, who conducted the post-mortem, estimated the time of death as not later than 2 am although it was more likely that death had occurred several hours earlier, at about 9 pm, when the girl was returning from the library. But no one had heard anything. No one had seen anything on the unlit road where only the occasional passing tramcar broke the darkness.

There was no certainty about Nellie's moves that evening. It was a foul winter's night, rainy and windy, and it seemed probable that she came back by tram from the Woolwich Arsenal main gates to Shooters Hill Road, a penny stage, which ended near where she lived. If she did that she would have walked down Well Hall Road, past the common on her left, to her home. On either side of the road at this point there were no houses. It was on that night a desolate spot, a lonely place for a girl.

Nellie Trew, attractive, quiet and home loving, was a studious youngster who had won an LCC scholarship, and who since leaving school had been working as a clerk at the Arsenal. She was devoted to her ailing mother and was always quickly home after work to help around the house. Her mother spoke of her affectionate character. 'We were not like mother and daughter: we were just two chums.' The nation, although still engaged in a war with millions of casualties, was nevertheless appalled by Nellie Trew's murder.

It was only when Chief Inspector Francis Carlin from Scotland Yard took charge of the investigation that progress was made. Carlin with his clipped moustache and grey hair is described as a neat man, always impeccably dressed with a formal wing collar and striped tie. Leonard Gribble, writing in The *Star*, suggested that he looked more like a solicitor than a detective. In spite of his inoffensive appearance, Carlin was 'the terror of the swell mobsmen' – in other words, he was one of those detectives that criminals hoped to steer clear of.

The detective was immediately interested in the button. It had apparently been fastened to a coat by a piece of wire about 1½ inches long, sharpened to a point at one end and fractured at the other, as if it had been broken off a woman's hat pin. It had been found 30 yards from the body. The white metal badge had been picked up 47 yards away in the other direction. It was a long shot but Carlin felt that they ought to be considered as definite clues. He had photographs and drawings of both published in the newspapers.

Carlin had a phone call from Tottenham Court Road police station on the morning the photographs appeared. A young man claimed to have recognised the cap badge as his own and had gone to the station to clarify matters. The man had said that he had sold the badge to a stranger on the tram that ran between Well Hall and Eltham. Previously he had worn it in his lapel, but only days earlier, on Friday last as a matter of fact, only a day before Nellie Trew was murdered, he had sold it for two shillings. The point was, the man said, that he wanted to ensure that he was not going to accused of something he had not done. He had been persuaded by his workmates who had seen him wearing the badge that he ought to go along to the police and clear matters up

A drawing of the badge discovered near the murder scene, as illustrated in the national press.

so that he didn't get into trouble. Carlin immediately sent for the statement.

The young man who had made the statement had an interesting background. Though now only 21, David Greenwood had joined the army in 1914 when he was seventeen. He had fought in France and in 1916 he had been buried alive after a shell exploded near him and a rescue party had had to dig him out. After that a Medical Panel had diagnosed shell shock and heart trouble and he had been invalided out of the army. Since 4th February, he had been working as a turner at the Hewson Manufacturing Company, just off Tottenham Court Road.

Greenwood gave his address as 13 Jupiter Terrace, a street that backed onto the common, only 100 yards from where the body had been found, and not far from Nellie Trew's home. But he was able to account for his movements on Saturday, 9th February. He had left work at one o'clock, he said, and went to Charing Cross where he had lunch at Lyons. Then he caught a train to Well Hall at three o'clock. He had a haircut and then caught the tram home and later, at about 4 pm, he went out to the public baths at Woolwich. He had returned home at 5 pm, eaten his tea and then had gone out again to Woolwich, this time to buy work overalls. It was on his way home on the tram that he had met a man who had noticed the badge in his lapel. The man, a total stranger, had asked if he could buy the badge as he had a son in the Leicesters. Greenwood had sold it to him for two shillings. He described the man as of medium height and middle aged. He had worn a black overcoat and bowler hat. 'His accent appeared to me as though he came from Belfast,' Greenwood said. 'I should say he was a man that had an outdoor life.'

Greenwood had reached home at about 7 pm and did not go out again until after 9.30 pm when he went yet again to Woolwich. There he had a tenpenny supper of bacon, potato and beans at the YMCA. He had left the YMCA at 11.20 pm and caught the last tram, reaching home at 11.45 pm.

Interesting. A badge found near Nellie Trew's body had, until the day of her death, belonged to a man who lived near the murder site. And that man had, only on the day before her death, sold it to a stranger he had met on a tram. Chief Inspector Carlin must have pondered on the odds of such a chance. He immediately sent his colleague, Inspector Brown, to Hewson's to collect Greenwood and bring him back to Scotland Yard.

Greenwood, a tall, gaunt figure, his overcoat hanging slackly on his bony frame, was with the Chief Inspector within an hour. Carlin chatted to him, roaming over the young man's background in the army, his service in an RAMC unit attached to the Leicesters. He learnt that the pale-faced man in front of him was in poor physical condition and that he was subject to fainting spells. And then conversation passed on to the statement Greenwood had made earlier in the day at Tottenham Court Road police station and as they spoke Carlin became aware that Greenwood's overcoat had no buttons. In every place save one, the threads showed where once there had been a button. But where the top button had been there was a small hole as though the button had been torn away. And how was it that there were no buttons? How had that come about? People do not normally wear overcoats with no buttons. Especially not in an English February. Carlin commented on the lack of buttons and the young man was clearly uncomfortable, muttering something about their not having been sewn on properly.

It is at this point that Carlin showed himself at his most decisive, acting on intuition. He asked Greenwood to wait in another room, no doubt apologising for the inconvenience. That done, he and Brown went off to Hewson's where the manager, John Gibson, confirmed that he had seen the badge in Greenwood's buttonhole. According to Gibson, the buttons on Greenwood's overcoat were like the one Carlin showed him. This information was supported by others among Greenwood's workmates. As for his coat, he always wore it buttoned up including the top button. The only odd thing was that the top button had been held in place with a piece of twisted wire instead of being sewn with thread. And some of these witnesses were certain that none of the buttons had been missing the day before Carlin's visit.

Anything else they had noticed? Yes, come to think of it, there had been a change in the way he behaved. Normally, he had appeared a bright and cheerful young chap but since the weekend he'd been rather quiet. And there had been a distinct falling off in his work. Frank Rabson, a charge hand at the works, considered that Greenwood's work was not efficient and that he appeared rather agitated. Aware of the young man's army experiences, he had assumed that he was unwell.

But that button, Carlin mused. Held on with wire. In this factory that made aeroplane parts they used wire. If the wire on the button came from here then it would suggest even more strongly that Greenwood might be more deeply involved in the murder than he had indicated.

Carlin went next into the workshops, inspecting short clips of wire that had come off the lathes. Unlike the wire on the button, none of these had one end sharpened to a point. Here, both ends of the wires had been snipped with cutters.

Carlin was told that Hewson's used small gauge Springfield wire made to a certain specification for use on aircraft. The manager said that no other factory was working with such wire because they were currently employed on a special government contract. Could he distinguish it from other wire, Carlin asked him. He could recognise it anywhere, came the answer. He could recognise it in the dark. Carlin decided to test his claim. When the manager was momentarily absent, Carlin placed five pieces of wire he had picked up in the workshop on the desk. Then he placed the wire from the button among them. When the manager returned Carlin challenged him to select the alien wire. But after scrutiny the manager was adamant. All six pieces came from his factory. When the foreman was called in for Carlin to put him through the same test he also was in no doubt that all six pieces came from Hewson's.

The two detectives had met Greenwood for the first time only an hour or two earlier, but as they left the factory they already believed that they knew the identity of their murderer. Now it was important to collect any other evidence from Greenwood's home and also to question his family. They would have seen the pictures of the regimental badge and button in the newspaper and might even now be preparing to save him, concocting an alibi for him, regardless of how they might feel about the crime.

Carlin and Brown took a taxi to Greenwood's home. They searched the bedroom he shared with his brother but found no bloodstained garments. Some family members were interviewed. But their accounts of what Greenwood had done on the night of the murder differed. His mother, May Greenwood, remembered that he had gone out without his overcoat, despite the windy, wet and cold night. She told the detectives that she had been worried that he would catch cold. After he came home, she said, he had come to her room and they had talked for a while. She had not noticed any blood on his clothes nor seen any signs of disturbed behaviour.

But Samuel Greenwood, his 16-year-old brother, had a different tale to tell. He said that he and his brother went to bed at about 9.30 pm. A sister's version of when he left the house differed from the mother's.

Another relative gave another account of the night. It did seem that, in the short time available to them, the family had colluded in their desperation to save Greenwood from the gallows. And Carlin thoroughly understood why this should be so. Years later he wrote, 'Let me be absolutely frank on the score of evidence from the relatives of any man charged with a crime, particularly that of murder, where his life is at stake. In cases of this nature, it is only natural that the mother, sisters and other relatives should do all they can to try to establish his innocence. It is not a case of telling falsehoods but showing that no two people see a thing alike. In the case of David Greenwood, I was concerned with only one thing. I had to bring him to justice and show that he was guilty. On the strength of the case I had built up out of that badge and button, I knew he had murdered Nellie Trew and there was no possible alibi which could show that he was wrongly accused.'

Returning to Scotland Yard, Carlin again spoke to Greenwood who asserted that on the day of the murder he went nowhere near the place where Nellie Trew had been attacked. Nor had he worn an overcoat that day. He repeated the account he had given earlier in his statement. Most of the evening, he said, he had spent at home but at ten o'clock he had gone out to the YMCA to get some supper. He was signing a second statement to that effect when there was a dramatic moment. While Greenwood was occupied with writing, Carlin had placed the coat button on his desk. Looking up from the document, Greenwood saw it. He picked it up and turned it over.

'If I say this is mine what will it mean?' he asked.

'That's something I can't tell you,' Carlin replied.

Greenwood was now clearly anxious. 'Very well,' he said. 'In that case, I won't say it.'

Shortly after this David Greenwood was charged with murder.

Greenwood appeared before Mr Justice Atkins at the Central Criminal Court on 24th April 1918. He pleaded not guilty.

Under questioning, Greenwood offered a feeble excuse for the absence of buttons on his coat. He said that he had used them to 'pack' the lathe but evidence was offered that 'packing' was always done with pieces of metal. Had a button been used for this purpose it would have been smashed to pieces. The prosecution argued that Greenwood took the other buttons off his coat only after the newspapers showed pictures of the one in police hands. He maintained that he had never liked the overcoat, which had been issued to him on his army discharge in 1917.

The Badge and Button Murder

The buttons, he said, were poorly sewn on and had come off easily. In any case, he reiterated that on the day of the murder he had not worn the coat.

But the evidence of the wire on the button was what clinched the case for the prosecution. Had it not been for that, perhaps the case would have collapsed.

Sir Travers Humphreys, who led for the prosecution, was to write later, 'When at the Bar, it was my practice, in my later years, to talk with the junior members of my chambers on such topics as circumstantial evidence. Greenwood's case was a favourite one on these occasions, when we found it interesting to discuss this problem: "If Greenwood had used thread instead of wire to fasten one of his overcoat buttons, would there have been enough evidence to justify a conviction?" '

Mr Slesser, the defence counsel, recognising that the circumstantial evidence against his client was so strong, made much of Greenwood's war service. He tried to get Sir Bernard Spilsbury to admit that a man of Greenwood's physical condition, a man discharged from the army with serious health problems, would have been unable to overpower a healthy young girl. Spilsbury refused to commit himself either way. He was, the great pathologist replied, unable to say that a man in such a condition would be unable to attack and overcome a girl.

It took the jury nearly three hours to find Greenwood guilty and when the verdict was announced there was an added recommendation for mercy because of the guilty man's youth, his good character and particularly his service to his country.

When asked by the judge if he had anything to say before sentence was passed, Greenwood declared: 'I am not guilty of this crime. I know absolutely nothing about it. I have never seen or spoken to Nellie Trew in my life.'

But then he added, most remarkably, 'I wish your Lordship, if possible, not to take any notice of the recommendation to mercy, as rather than have the disgrace of this crime on me, I would pay the full penalty.' He was sentenced to death and was due to hang on 3rd May.

Greenwood's father conducted a campaign to petition the King for a reprieve. The petition emphasised the circumstantial nature of the evidence against his son. After all, the badge and the button, the principal items of evidence, were both of common enough types. Furthermore, the jury had taken nearly three hours to reach their verdict, indication enough of their uncertainty, as was their strong recommendation for mercy. There was, the petition said, no proper direction by the judge on some important matters, particularly with reference to the badge. The jury had not been advised to consider the fact that there were many such badges in existence, especially in the neighbourhood of Eltham. Furthermore, the button and badge were found in different places, on ground trampled over by many people. Was there absolute proof that these two items belonged to Greenwood?

The appeal was dismissed. Although the evidence was admittedly circumstantial, the appeal judges said it was sufficient to justify the guilty verdict. But on the eve of the execution the Home Secretary intervened and Greenwood was reprieved. He was sentenced to life imprisonment. Greenwood served fifteen years in jail and was released in 1933 at the age of 36.

Of David Greenwood's guilt there can be no doubt. But it was a nice point made by Travers Humphreys. What would have happened had there been no wire attached to the button? Would the prosecution case have then seemed so strong?

And another question occurs: Would the jury have added their strong recommendation for mercy if the defence had not so forcefully drawn attention to Greenwood's army service: his joining up at the age of seventeen, his being in action on the Western Front, his narrow escape from being buried alive and finally the ill-health associated with his ordeals in the military?

And yet another question: Should battlefield experiences be used to excuse criminal behaviour?

THE RUCKINGE
BUNGALOW MURDER

That's what Mrs Salvage must have liked about living in the country. People were so kind. They were helpful, trustworthy. This afternoon she'd been to down to Ashford for a few hours and had just got on the 7.40 pm bus home to Ruckinge and the driver, Fred Hill, told her he'd been to her place earlier in the day, sometime after five o'clock. Somebody had given him a basket of strawberries to deliver to her because she was on his route. He'd called at the bungalow and he'd knocked at the door and he'd shouted and whistled and there'd been no reply. He'd even gone round to the back garden but no one had answered. Anyway, he told Mrs Salvage, he'd left the strawberries on her kitchen table with a note. Then he had gone on his way with his passengers.

Such chance encounters always served to confirm in Mrs Salvage's mind that she had been wise to come to Ruckinge. For a while after they left London, she and her husband had lived in Walmer and then, after his death, young Arthur had given up the Merchant Navy and had come to live with her. She hadn't known quite what he would want to do when he came ashore and he'd been as uncertain as young men so often were. Anyway, they'd finally decided that he could become a poultry farmer and she'd bought the bungalow, Sunningdale, and Arthur's chickens. He seemed happy enough, settled in the village, playing cricket for the local team. As for Mrs Salvage herself, she had enough to keep her occupied, what with the choir and various church functions. On her way home on the bus that summer evening of 1931 Mrs May Salvage, fit, active and, at 50, relatively young, must have believed herself one of the happiest women alive. Her happiness was not to last. From the moment she stepped off the bus, it was all to change.

As soon as she went into the house Arthur told her the news. One of the village girls had gone missing. Nobody had seen her for the last four hours or so. People were out looking for her. It was 11-year-old Ivy Godden. Mrs Salvage's heart sank. She knew Ivy well. She was in her choir. The child lived only half a mile away, up at Bromley Green.

Arthur told his mother that he had seen Peter Godden, Ivy's 13-year-old brother, earlier. Apparently Peter and Ivy had come home from school at about four o'clock and twenty minutes or so later Peter had gone to the woods with a wheelbarrow to collect wood. He had passed Arthur at the gate and they had said hello to each other. Then, at 5.15 pm, while Arthur was planting cabbages in the kitchen garden, Peter had come over to him again. Was he going to cricket, Arthur had asked him? But Peter had other things on his mind. It was Ivy. She was missing. She hadn't been seen for three-quarters of an hour. Had Arthur seen her? She'd left the house at about 4.30 pm, shortly after Peter. He had expected her to catch him up because she was going to help him collect wood. In fact, he had caught a glimpse of her along the road behind him but she had then disappeared from view. But Arthur hadn't seen her. If he did, he told the anxious boy, he would certainly let him know. And if he wanted any help to look for her he just needed to ask.

By the time May Salvage had reached the house the search for the child was still on but no one recalled seeing Ivy apart from one near neighbour, Alice Foster, who could remember seeing her walking towards May Cross and Packing Wood, which would take her past Sunningdale, the Salvage bungalow. But there were no other sightings. With a neighbour and Peter, Mrs Godden searched and searched but could find no trace of the girl. On her way to the woods, at about 5.40 pm, she spoke to Arthur Salvage, still in the front of his house. He enquired if Ivy had been found. He'd be glad to help, he said, if he was needed.

It was ten o'clock when Ivy's father, another Peter, came home from work. He was a woodman and he had been working late. This was the first he had heard of his daughter's disappearance. He immediately telephoned the police and began searching the woods. He called on the Salvages but Arthur could not help. Yes, he had seen Peter and Mrs Godden but he had certainly not seen Ivy that afternoon. Godden, joined by other villagers, continued looking for the missing child.

The next day, Saturday 4th July, there was an organised search of the area by 75 people, some of whom scoured the woods and lanes throughout the night. Among the searchers was 23-year-old Arthur Salvage.

The police had been alerted on the Friday evening and were on the look-out for a girl wearing a brown felt hat, a light brown silk dress and carrying a cricket bat that had been fashioned out of the wooden lid of the family's copper boiler. But the police were used to youngsters going off and then reappearing within hours. In the early evening, after a day's fruitless search, the local policeman reported to his superiors: 'We have made inquiries and in all probability the girl has left home because of rows and trouble – there appears to have been a tiff between Godden and her parents last night.' But the constable's scepticism was not shared by local people, who were determined to go on looking for Ivy the following day.

While the search was concentrated on Barn Woods, just at the rear of Sunningdale, and behind the mission hall, Ivy's uncle, John Godden, noticed a patch of ground where shrubs had been recently planted but had wilted. Scraping away the soil, he found a sack and when this was cut open he saw what looked like a brown dress. He knew the search was over, knew what lay under the ground. The police were immediately informed and a police surgeon summoned to the site.

Beneath a hastily dug grave, the body of Ivy Godden, a strong, well-developed child who was above average in height and weight, was covered with sacking and tied with a rope looped around her ankles and neck. Her dress was drawn up under her armpits and her cotton knickers were round her knees. The homemade cricket bat was wedged between her right arm and her body. Her face and neck were severely bruised. Sir Bernard Spilsbury, who conducted the post-mortem, thought she had died of shock caused by the beating she had received.

Detective Chief Superintendent Avery and Superintendent Robertson, both of the Kent Constabulary, were now responsible for the investigation. At this stage Avery interviewed several local people simply as witnesses. Among those interviewed was Arthur Salvage, who made a lengthy statement. Did Avery already suspect Salvage of the brutal murder? It seems so because although Salvage was making a routine witness statement, the policeman felt the need to caution him in reply to a question regarding the clothing he had worn on the Friday of the murder.

Naturally the officers were interested in Salvage as the grave was only a hundred yards or so from Sunningdale. Was it not odd that a grave should be dug so close to the bungalow? Was there not a risk that whoever dug the grave might be seen by the occupants? But one of the

Discovery of the body, Illustrated Police News, *9 July 1931*.

occupants, Mrs Salvage, was in Ashford at the time Ivy disappeared. And Arthur Salvage could have had an opportunity … but it was only surmise. But what about the rope with which Ivy's body had been tied? In the lean-to shed at the side of the bungalow there were similar lengths of rope. And the sacking in which the body was wrapped was certainly similar to that which was nailed to the side of the goat house. Neither of these items was proof of any kind but they were enough to provoke thought. Rope and sacking were sent off for further investigation.

At three o'clock on the Monday morning, officers from the West Sussex Constabulary arrived with their bloodhound, Herold. Armed with flash lamps and lanterns they began a search for further evidence around the area where the body had been found.

Herold was taken to the grave and given the sacking and the dead girl's shoes and stockings to smell. Then, given the order to 'sniff and seek', the dog set off, working a trail across a potato patch and through the undergrowth to a path which led to the Salvage bungalow. With his muzzle to the ground, he crossed a small bridge, and then stopped at the front door. His handler took him back to the starting point and, again, Herold returned to Sunningdale. Once more the dog was taken back to Ivy's grave, once more allowed to smell the sacking, the shoes and stockings, and then a third time he ended up at the bungalow.

When the Salvages came to the door, the policemen were invited inside but the bloodhound refused to go beyond the front step. His handler explained that the Salvages' two dogs were barking inside and that Herold, typical of his breed, was too shy to go into the house.

But Herold was not too shy to go to Mrs Salvage. He approached her as she stood at the front door, sniffing her hand. She bent over and he allowed her to pat him. But Herold did not go near Arthur Salvage. Of course, that might not be conclusive but it seemed to convince the police officers that there was some detailed questioning required at Sunningdale. Perhaps Arthur was too well scrubbed; possibly his clothing was too well washed.

In the course of the day, the rope from the body was compared with a length of rope in the lean-to garden shed at Sunningdale. A rope manufacturer at Maidstone confirmed they were very similar. The County Analyst confirmed that both the sacking on the body and that taken from the goat house carried identical goat hairs.

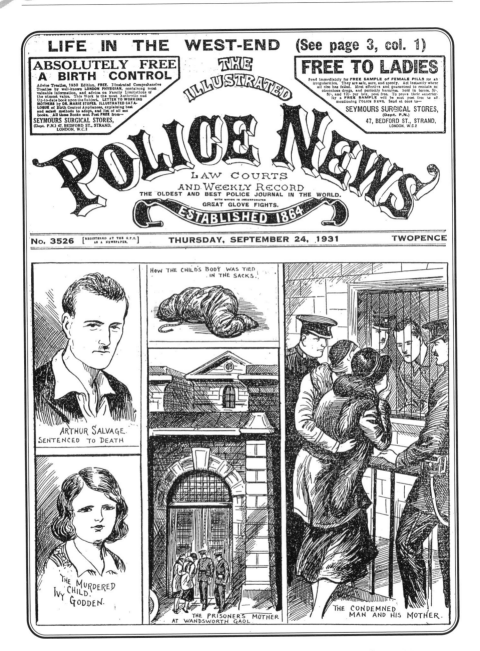

The story of the murder, Illustrated Police News, *24 September 1931.*

At nine o'clock in the evening Detective Chief Superintendent Avery decided to arrest Salvage. On his arrival at the bungalow the young man was absent. His mother informed the policeman that Henry Flint, a solicitor from Chatham and hired by the *Daily Sketch*, was already speaking to her son, offering to represent him free of charge. When Salvage returned from his discussions with Flint it was ten o'clock. The two men had walked round the local cricket field for hours discussing options.

Now under arrest, Salvage was taken to the police station at Ashford. Once there, there was little delay. Salvage confessed to the crime almost immediately. Speaking to Chief Superintendent Avery, he said, 'I want to be quite straight with you for the sake of my mother. I did this. I killed Ivy. I don't want any defence.' Salvage was deeply upset and burst into tears. Turning to Superintendent Robertson who was also in the room he said, 'I am sorry, Mr Robertson.'

This moment was crucial to the later hearings. Did Avery at this point caution Salvage? Did he ask him if he understood exactly what it was he was saying? Avery was always adamant that the tearful Salvage was aware of the implications of what he was saying.

Salvage wrote a confession in 62 words: 'I was waiting outside the front gate when I saw Ivy Godden coming along. I asked her into the place and there did this. I carried her out of the place and took her down into the wood and buried her. This all happened before Peter Godden junior came to see me and asked if I had seen her. That is all.'

Sometime after this Henry Flint turned up as Salvage's legal representative. When he was asked if he wished to see him, Salvage responded, 'Definitely not.'

Remorse perhaps persuaded him to confess to the crime. The following morning a telegram arrived from Flint. The accused man rejected this overture too. 'I don't want any defence,' he told the police officers. 'It is no good. I killed her in my bedroom when mother was out. I buried her that night. Her hat I buried in the garden patch.' And in response to the telegram, he said, 'Don't come to court.'

But Flint did come to the magistrates' court for Mrs Salvage was anxious that her son should have professional representation, backed by a national newspaper. The Sketch might employ a rather seedy solicitor but he was extremely competent and that was all that a mother could want. And now, only hours after making his confession, under the neat, persuasive arguments of Henry Flint, Salvage had retracted every word. And the focus of Flint's attack – for a defence solicitor does attack – was on the way in which Arthur Salvage had been persuaded so quickly to confess to a murder which he had not committed. Flint's approach did not, however, prevent the magistrates from referring the case to the Assize court but once it was there, Salvage's defence would follow the same course as that laid down by Flint.

The murder of Ivy Godden was widely reported. There was massive public interest and many newspapers printed verbatim accounts of the proceedings with no details spared. There were scores of sightseers outside the Old Bailey on each of the three days of the trial, which opened on 14th September 1931, before Mr Justice MacNaughten. Mr J.D. Cassels appeared for the prosecution and Mr Marston Garsia for the defence.

The case for the Crown was summed up neatly by Mr Cassels. 'In the submission of the prosecution,' he said, 'Ivy Godden was murdered in the bungalow on the afternoon of the 3rd July by blows, either with a fist or the bat found with her dead body buried in the wood, and it was committed by the one and only man in residence at that bungalow at the time.' Among the incriminating evidence were fragments of a hat, burnt in a small fire in the garden at Sunningdale, and a bloodstain on Arthur Salvage's bed. The sacking and the rope were also presented in evidence.

There were occasions of unintended humour in court, which momentarily lightened the grim tale as it unfolded. Once, Mr Garsia asked Detective Constable Heathfield: 'How deep was the grave?'

'About 16 inches,' the constable replied.

'How long will it take to dig a grave like that?' Mr Garsia asked, hoping in some way to suggest that whoever had dug it, Arthur Salvage had not sufficient time to do so.

But back came the stonewall answer, which did not advance the defence case one inch. 'I've never dug a grave, sir.'

Mrs Godden had previously said that when she was seeking her daughter near to Sunningdale she had thought she heard her calling out to her in a feeble voice. 'I don't know whether it was a voice really or a presentiment,' she had said in the magistrates' court. 'It immediately made me go out to search for her. I knew there was something wrong when she did not come home, as every mother would.'

Now at the Assizes Mr Garsia asked her, 'What is your feeling about it now?'

J D Cassels, KC.

'That it was a presentiment. I don't think I did hear it really.' But Garsia was to argue later that Mrs Godden had heard her daughter cry out. It was no presentiment because her son, Peter, also heard it. But, said Mr Garsia, the cry could not have come from the Salvage's bungalow because his neighbour would surely have heard it.

It was Garsia's aim to persuade the court that Salvage had been wheedled and cajoled into making a confession at a time when, in a state of utter collapse, he was unfit to make any sensible decision. He had not even been cautioned, the defence claimed. Superintendent Robertson denied putting his arm round the weeping Salvage's shoulder on the way to Ashford. No, said the officer, he had not said to him, 'Cheer up, old man.' And he further rejected the suggestion that he had said, 'I am speaking to you as man to man and not in my official capacity ... Speaking like that, I'd really advise you to admit it all.'

In the witness box Salvage denied the charge. He admitted that he had been distressed after his arrest and he described how Robertson had told him it would be better for his mother and himself to confess to the murder. He was cross-examined by Mr Cassels about this:

Q: When you said you had killed Ivy, was that true?
A: No.
Q: Why did you tell a lie so much against your own interest?
A: Because I was fed up.
Q: What had fed you up?
A: The way they had treated mother and myself.

Mrs Salvage also had her turn in the witness box. What she most clearly remembered was her son's reaction when they heard that people were discussing the possibility that Ivy had been murdered. He had said to her, 'Poor little girl. I cannot think who would want to kill Ivy. She was such a nice child.'

As for the burnt hat found in the garden and which the prosecution asserted had belonged to Ivy Godden, Mrs Salvage said that on the Tuesday or the Wednesday before the girl's disappearance she had burned a variety of rubbish including three of her own old hats. Furthermore it would have been impossible for her son to sneak out of the bungalow on the night of the murder in order to bury the body under cover of darkness. She was a light sleeper, she said, and she would have heard him. According to Salvage's earlier statement, the body had been buried before 5.15 pm when Peter Godden had come to ask him if he had seen his sister. This may suggest that even at the time of the trial the police were uncertain of when exactly the burial took place.

Mr Garsia asked the jury what compelling and substantial evidence there was against his client. What was the motive? The prosecution had not suggested a motive. Had it not been for the confession the jury would never consider his client guilty. But that confession, the very nub of the case, had been made by a highly distraught man whose emotions had been played on by two senior police officers. He wondered why confessions were made in a police station. Was there some specific atmosphere in a police station that inclined people to confess? It might not seem very logical for his client to have claimed he was tired of so many questions but was it not possible? 'A man in his position who had not committed the crime might say: "I am sick and tired of this. I will say anything and nothing will happen because I have not done it." '

Summing up, Mr Justice MacNaughten reminded the jury that it was not incumbent on the prosecution to establish any motive. He was not impressed by the defence's claims that the police officers had made 'inducements' to the accused to persuade him to confess. It had been alleged that Superintendent Robertson had said, 'It would be better for your mother and yourself if you confessed.' But, his Lordship asked, how could it be better for his mother or himself to confess that he had done this dreadful deed? It was difficult to see, assuming the prisoner was innocent, how he could do other than claim his innocence.

After a withdrawal of only 30 minutes, the jury returned a verdict of guilty. Arthur Salvage was condemned to death, the sentence to be carried out on 6th October.

There was no appeal. Instead, Mr Garsia focused the attention of the Home Office on his client's mental condition. A medical inquiry was ordered and Salvage was certified insane. The death sentence was respited and he was sent to Broadmoor.

Salvage's mother, still living in the bungalow, was overjoyed to hear of the respite, the news of which came to her in a long telegram from the Home Secretary. 'But do not be too sure about Broadmoor,' she said. 'I know on what grounds the decision has been granted but it is a secret. My son is not mad. There is much more to come yet for the mystery is not solved. Some day there is going to be a bombshell to surprise everyone. Does that mean I believe my son is innocent? Of course I do. I have never lost faith. What mother would? But it is not only a mother's point of view. Even if I had been on the jury I should still have believed him to be not guilty.'

But there was no bombshell. Despite her confidence in her son, Arthur Salvage was never released. The Daily Mail revealed something of his background. Salvage was from a well-connected family and had the advantages of a comfortable home and a good education at the Simon Langton School in Canterbury. However, he had let the family down; after several convictions for petty theft he was sent to Borstal. Eventually he joined the Merchant Navy but then came ashore to live with his mother. At Ruckinge he became well known. He was a keen cricketer and attended church regularly as he did on the day that Ivy Godden's body was found.

Salvage was also suspected of the murder of Louisa Steele, whose nude, mutilated body was found at Blackheath in January 1931. Two other Blackheath women and others in Hove were thought to have been assaulted by him about the same time. He was first interviewed by Superintendent Cooper, one of the Big Five, who was in charge of the Blackheath murder. Salvage denied responsibility for the murder but later he wrote to the Superintendent admitting that he had murdered Louisa Steele. Although he did discuss the crime with Cooper, the police could not find sufficient evidence to bring the case to court.

Arthur Salvage died in Broadmoor. Of his guilt in the Ivy Godden case there is no doubt. But what of Louisa Steele? Her murder was never solved. Was Arthur Salvage just boasting, simply attention seeking, when he claimed to have killed her? Was he glorying in the reputation of being a murderer? Or was Arthur Salvage an even more frightening resident of Ruckinge that anyone had ever suspected?

THE TIME FACTOR

It was an ordinary sort of day, the kind of day that gets lost, the kind that's never remembered. It was the kind of day that we all experience for much of the time. For most of us, the ordinary days outnumber those that stick in the mind. So 10th July 1939 started for the Jacksons much like any other. There they were in their home in Sholden, the modest detached house in London Road that they named Eastwood, where they had lived since they married four years earlier, the unassuming home that this very ordinary couple – ordinary in the sense that most of us are ordinary – were buying on a mortgage.

So how ordinary a day was it? Let's hear Sidney Jackson's own words. 'Today', he says, 'my wife and I got up at 7.50 and followed the morning routine. Whilst I was shaving a roadman came to the door and asked my wife for some water. I did not see the man, but overheard the conversation while I was in the bathroom. The time would be about 8.10. Shortly afterwards we breakfasted together. I had Kelloggs flakes and a boiled egg. She had Kelloggs and bread and marmalade. When I left for work at 8.33 my wife was still eating her breakfast. I remember the time because I looked at the clock just before I left and then the green Horne's bus went by as it always does about that time.

'When I left home I kissed her and went out by the front door. It's the last I saw of my wife. She was sitting at the table in the kitchen and feeding the dog, which was in its basket under the table. She was then alone in the house. This morning my wife put on some old clothing because she was going to wash. I cannot remember exactly what she was wearing.'

There's a feeling that this household runs like clockwork, this morning, every morning. And you can't get more ordinary than Kelloggs, egg, toast and marmalade. It's Monday so naturally it's washing day and Margaret is dressed ready to make a start once she has finished her breakfast and fed the dog. Nor has this responsible hard-working 26-year-old woman been idle since she got up. While

Sidney was shaving she went up the garden and chopped sticks ready for the boiler. And then there comes a knock at the door: it's one of the men tarring the road. They are working on a job on the corner where New Road and London Road meet. Margaret opens the door. Can he and his mates have a drop of hot water for their tea, the roadman asks her? She goes off to the kitchen with his can. The workman wonders if he has made a good choice coming to this house to ask for water. The dog was barking before the door opened and then no sooner was it opened than out it dashed, a little Irish terrier. It was quite alarming. It really worried him, that little dog. It quite went at him. Then his mistress got him by the collar and took him inside the house.

By the time Sidney comes down from the bathroom the workman has gone. He has his breakfast and, shortly afterwards, off he goes on his bicycle, passing the workmen drinking their tea. He has been working at Betteshanger colliery as a wages clerk for the past nine years. It's only a short ride, no more than half a mile, and on the way he meets one of his colleagues and they cycle along together to their workplace.

Back at Eastwood there's not much activity. You'd expect more on a washing day. At 9.50 am when the milkman calls there is no reply to his knock on the door. He tries three times to get an answer but save for the dog, which barks from behind the door, there is still no response. The dog, it seems, has the run of the house this morning but as he moves away into another room, somewhere into the back of the house, the sound of his barking fades. The milkman gives up and continues his round. Mrs Jackson must have forgotten that he'd be calling for his money this morning.

And the July morning passes. The roadmen outside go on with their tarring. Neighbours potter about in their gardens. People pass up and down the road. And then, for Sidney Jackson, it's lunchtime. He always goes home for lunch. There's no canteen at Betteshanger.

But there's something strange here. As soon as he gets in the house he wonders what can be wrong. The place is always so well organised. But the table hasn't been set yet. He only has an hour for lunch and usually Margaret has everything ready. There's no sign of a meal. The breakfast dishes are still on the draining board. What on earth is going on? He hears the dog barking in the front sitting room. He opens the sitting room door and the dog runs out to greet him. But Margaret's not in there. Perhaps she locked him in the sitting room

DOG MAY SEND VILLA SLAYER TO THE SCAFFOLD

Scotland Yard Men's Dramatic New Clues

(Fro....... ....wn Correspondent)

....rday. — Scotland Yard officers .... murder here of Mrs. Margaret ....ve discovered four clues which, ...ead her slayer to the scaffold.

....y novel, " **The Man in a Corner,**" ....led pair of corsets, and saliva ....d tan mongrel dog.

London, too, are the digestive from Mrs. Jackson's body. It is ....to a minute when she had her ....il, which was with her husband. ....ey Jackson, before he went off

....sible to tell by analysis almost ....minute the murder was com- ....1 the stage at which the pro- ....stion stopped.

....RD " SUSPICIOUS

MRS. MARGARET NEWTON JACKSON.

SIX MEN IN CAR

MOTORIST SAYS HE WAS ATTACKED

EARLY MORNING SCENE IN

Extract from the News of the World, *16 July 1939.*

as she sometimes does if someone calls and she thinks he might be a nuisance.

Jackson goes to the foot of the stairs, calling up to the bedroom. 'Carrots,' he shouts, using his pet name for her, probably because her hair has a tinge of red in it. 'Carrots!' But there's no reply and so now he goes upstairs, first popping his head into the back bedroom. She's not there either.

She is in the main bedroom. She is lying face down on the bed, her feet by the pillows. He speaks to her, calls her name. He touches her on the back and she seems rigid and cold. Then he touches her left shoulder and that is slightly warmer. He takes in the scene. She is almost naked, her clothing torn and all rucked up round her neck, her face buried in the eiderdown. Her hair is matted with blood. He does not know what to do.

The above account of the discovery of the body, which would later be challenged, comes from two statements made by Sidney Jackson, the first on the day of the murder, the second on 22nd July when, accompanied by his brother, he voluntarily visited the police station at Deal. This was, he said, to fill in any gaps. He had thought of one or two other things that might be helpful to the police.

After discovering Margaret in the bedroom, Jackson had run out of the house across to the Doubledays. Unlike the majority of people, they had a telephone. In answer to his knocking Mrs Doubleday opened the door. He was in 'terrible trouble', he told her. Margaret needed a doctor. Could she telephone for one? And the police, he thought they should come too. Would she also phone the police?

While Mrs Doubleday was contacting the doctor and the police, Jackson dashed home. He was, he would later say, unwilling to believe that his wife was dead. He went up to the bedroom, moving the eiderdown from her face and seeing the extent of her injuries for the first time. Then he went downstairs again. Mrs Doubleday came into the kitchen and gave him a dose of sal volatile to calm him down.

Detective Sergeant Chamberlain from Sandwich arrived on the scene very quickly, within minutes of the telephone call. He took in the fact that nothing downstairs had been disturbed. The detective noted the crockery on the kitchen draining board and, in front of the fireplace, the bucket, already filled with water, ready for the Monday wash.

The only indication of any struggle was in the bedroom, where the body lay face downward on the bed. There was a wound to the left temple and blood on the face and on the eiderdown. Margaret Jackson had been forcibly stripped. Her torn underclothing lay on the floor by the bed as did her apron, its straps torn.

The light at the top of the stairs was on and between the bathroom and bedroom doors there was a stepladder. It wasn't normally there, Jackson told the detective. It was kept along with the deck chairs and the tennis rackets in the little downstairs storeroom off the kitchen. They only used the stepladder when they wanted something from the roof space and it hadn't been there when he left the house. Perhaps his wife had brought it upstairs, Chamberlain suggested. She would never do that, Jackson told him. She never went into the roof space. If they wanted anything from up there, he brought the stepladder and went up to bring down whatever was needed. In any event, there was nothing up there apart from some suitcases and an old rag rug. And why was the landing light on? Because there was no light up in the roof space.

And another odd thing: at the end of the passage upstairs, the lavatory door was open. They never left it open. Had Margaret been on her way out of the lavatory and been confronted by the intruder? But then, of course, murderers themselves often need to use lavatories on the completion of their work.

There was no sign of a forced entry. The front door was firmly closed with a Yale lock. There was only one entrance to the property and that was through the front gate. The long back garden was bounded on one side by a neighbour's fence. On the other side and at the back was an impenetrable hedge. Whoever had come in must have entered through the kitchen door, which led from the garden. This door was always unlocked.

There had been complaints about tramps in the area and it might have been that one of them had broken in, but nothing appeared to have been stolen. There was a ladies' gold wristwatch in full view in the bedroom. A sixpenny piece lay on the carpet.

But what about the dog? It was said to bark whenever anyone approached the front door. It was fiercely protective of Margaret. Sidney Jackson admitted that it even went for him on occasion, barking, snarling, and tugging at his trousers. He was a good housedog, the kind of dog that warned off potential intruders, a dog that some people called vicious. One of the neighbours was to say, 'That is one of the strangest things about it. The dog would not allow anyone to enter the house if they seemed suspicious. Yet he made no sound.' And so, if no one had disturbed the dog that morning, was it not possible that it was Sidney who had murdered his wife? But of course, the dog had barked on two occasions, once when the roadman had called for hot water and later when the milkman came to the door. Perhaps the neighbours had become so accustomed to the barking that the noise no longer registered. Or then again, what if an assumed friend, someone the dog had known well, had called at the house sometime during that morning? Perhaps in that circumstance the dog did no more than wag its tail, never suspecting what was to follow.

At the inquest on the Wednesday after the murder, Sir Bernard Spilsbury described the findings of his three-hour post-mortem. He had at first thought that Margaret Jackson had died of head injuries but had revised his opinion. Although there was a head wound, the cause of death was strangulation. There was recent bruising to the legs, arms and thighs but she had not been raped though some bruising to the

Sir Bernard Spilsby, Home Office pathologist, Punch.

groin suggested that there had been an attempt. Spilsbury thought that she had been rendered unconscious by fierce punches to the face combined with hitting the back of her head on a hard surface as she fell. Unable to resist, she had then been strangled. Spilsbury based this judgement on the fact that the injuries to the neck were relatively slight. As Margaret's stomach was nearly full, containing about 10 ounces of partly digested food, death, in his opinion, had occurred within 15 to 20 minutes of the time she had eaten breakfast.

It was not surprising that in the course of their enquiries the police should pay attention to Sidney Jackson and his wife. But from what witnesses said they were two young people deeply devoted to each other. 'They were an ideal couple,' reported one, 'and I cannot think of anyone who disliked them.' Jackson himself turned out to be a man of exemplary character. They were a quiet pair with few friends, not because they were in any way unpleasant but because they were retiring. 'We kept ourselves to ourselves,' Jackson told the police. They belonged to the colliery tennis club but did not attend any associated social functions. At home the only visitors were Jackson's brother Wilfred and his wife who lived nearby. 'My wife had no men friends and spent her time in my company always when I was free,' Jackson said in his first statement. Otherwise, she busied herself about the house and garden. She was a mild-mannered woman who never lost her temper. In this first statement he said he doubted her ability to put up any resistance to an intruder but in his second statement he was of the opposite view. Yes, he said, she probably would have tried to give a good account of herself.

Jackson's change of view of her ability to try to defend herself might have been one of the factors that were to lead to his arrest. The investigators might have reasoned that on the day of the murder Jackson showed no visible signs of having been in a struggle with his wife. Was that because she had been unable to put up a fight? And was Jackson now suggesting to the police as an afterthought that she would have resisted enough to scratch or bruise her attacker and that they ought to be seeking someone who had shown signs of being in a struggle? And what about the dog? When the milkman called it had barked behind the door and had seemed to have the run of the house. Yet when Jackson came home he said that the dog was locked in the front sitting room. Did they begin to believe that Jackson had left the dog to roam free in the house after perhaps murdering his wife in an unpremeditated attack? And had Jackson then, arriving home at 1 pm, pretended that the dog had been in the sitting room? Was he hoping to mislead the police into thinking that the murderer must have been in the house after the milkman's visit?

But it was the time factor and the lack of barking that inclined the police to think that Sidney Jackson was responsible for his wife's death. Late on the Friday afternoon of 11th August, as he left work, he was arrested by Detective Superintendent Stuchfield and Superintendent Wheatley, both of Kent Constabulary, accompanied by Chief Inspector Salisbury of Scotland Yard. 'You know us,' Stuchfield said to Jackson. 'At 3 pm on 10th July I saw the body of your wife, Margaret Newton Jackson, lying on a bed at your house. Enquiries have been made respecting her death and as a result of these inquiries I am going to take you into custody and charge you with the murder of your wife.'

Jackson was charged at Sandwich police station. 'I think the charge is ridiculous,' he told Stuchfield. 'I realise that the police have had many difficulties and I have kept away from them for that reason. I am not satisfied with what the police have done to catch the man or woman who committed the murder.'

The next day he was taken to Canterbury Sessions House and, at a special sitting of the St Augustine's bench of magistrates, charged with murder. Mr E.G. Robey (son of George Robey, the celebrated music hall star) appeared for the prosecution. Mr J.A. Davis represented Sidney Jackson.

There were perhaps many who thought that Sidney Jackson had a case to answer. At the inquest, only 48 hours after the murder, the deputy coroner, Mr A.K. Mowll, proposing an adjournment, advised the jury, 'When you go away this afternoon do not consider in your own minds who was likely to have caused this death. Keep an open mind.'

There were other court hearings on 17th August, 29th August and 15th September. The adjournments were attributed to the international situation, for war was imminent when Jackson first appeared before the magistrates, and by the conclusion of the case, war had been declared.

The case before the magistrates hinged principally on time. The police had no doubt that when the milkman called at 9.50 a.m. Margaret Jackson was already dead. The only time the dog was heard was when he knocked at the door. The conclusion seemed obvious.

But the real question was: could Sidney Jackson have murdered his wife before leaving for work? He left the house on his own admission at 8.33 am. One of the workmen said that he saw him leave at about 8.30 as did a man standing at the nearby bus-stop. This time was also confirmed by the colleague who cycled to work with Jackson and who swore that his manner was much as usual. So if Jackson did kill his wife, it was done in the quarter of an hour or so between 8.15 am when the workman asked Margaret for hot water and 8.33 am.

Robey argued that the evidence was persuasive enough for the magistrates to think an Assize jury would convict Jackson. Not only were there the findings of Sir Bernard Spilsbury, the pathologist, but in reply to questions from the prosecution, Dr Fraser of Eastry, who had arrived at Eastwood at 4.30 pm on the day of the murder, said that he thought that death had occurred 8 to 10 hours beforehand. In other words death had occurred between 6.30 am and 8.30 am.

Q: Can you form any opinion as to when that meal, whatever it was, had been taken before death?

A: I'd formed the opinion that it would have taken approximately 30 minutes for the food to have reached that point.

Q: I suppose it follows that when death supervenes, the digestive process ceases?

A: Almost entirely.

In brief, because digestion was not complete, the doctor believed the murder took place sometime shortly after breakfast. More or less what Spilsbury had said.

For the defence, Mr Davis then cross-examined Dr Fraser.

Q: Talking about 8 to 10 hours. It is impossible to say accurately within half an hour?

A: It is from external observation.

Q: Of course it was upon external observation you based your opinion of 8 to 10 hours?

A: My first opinion.

Q: So far as the examination of the stomach contents were concerned you say that in your view the meal had started half an hour before it reached that point?

A: Yes.

And now Davis very gently bangs one nail into the prosecution case.

Q: Therefore, if she had not started her meal until after 8.15 am she probably would not have died until after 8.45 am.
A: Yes, that is so.

All of which contributes to Jackson's alibi as at 8.45 am he was arriving at work with a colleague.

Dr Milne of Walmer saw the body just after 1.30 pm on 10th July. Margaret Jackson had then been dead for some hours. The doctor had also been present at the post-mortem. He believed that the digestive process had taken under half an hour from the commencement of the meal. Under questioning by Mr Davis, however, he was rather less certain, refusing now to tie down his assessment of the time of death to a matter of ten minutes. That, he said, would be too precise an estimate.

And even the great Spilsbury, who assessed the time of death at about 15 to 20 minutes from the time of the meal, was forced to admit that he could not be too dogmatic on the matter of the timing. Mr Davis asked him, 'Would the process of digesting the food take into account the five minutes that intervened before death took place after strangulation?'

'Yes,' the pathologist conceded.

'If she had a meal at 8.15 am or 8.20 am, it comes to this, does it not, that you cannot say other than it is possible she died before 8.35.'

'I cannot say that it is more than a possibility.'

But men ought not to be hanged on mere possibilities. It was this successful challenge to the experts' claims that death possibly occurred at a time when Sidney Jackson was in the house that finally made up the minds of the magistrates. In their view, they said, there was no prima facie case to offer against Jackson.

And Sidney Jackson walked free.

So who killed Margaret Jackson in so brutal a fashion on 10th July 1939? Was it, as the family always believed, the one-time friendly neighbour who had climbed over the common back-garden fence as he frequently did and entered the house through the unlocked door to the kitchen? Had he gone there, shortly after Jackson's departure, on a harmless errand? Had he wanted perhaps to borrow something, a case, say, from the roof space? Had Margaret told him to take the ladder upstairs? And had he then suddenly decided that he wanted more than just a case? Had he been unable to control himself once he found himself upstairs with her? Ironic if that was so. Ironic if it should be a friend of two people who normally kept themselves to themselves.

Or was it a tramp?

Or was Jackson fortunate to find a lawyer who could so easily lay waste the claims of the medical experts?

THE GREAT ESCAPE

When 18-year-old Caroline Trayler failed to return to her home in Sussex Road on the evening of Sunday, 13th June 1943, her parents reported her absence to the police at Folkestone. When by the following day there was no sign of her, the police began a systematic search. They made extensive enquiries throughout the town; they looked in backyard sheds, deserted houses, and empty shops. They trawled through bombsites and recreation grounds. But the hours passed and they had no luck. Then on the Thursday morning, the fourth day of the search, PC Lewis, checking vacant premises on his beat, inspected a one-time greengrocer's shop, unoccupied for the past two years, at 94 Ford Road. The outside door was ajar. The constable found himself in what had been the living quarters of the shop. On the floor, in a passageway, were a blue suede shoe and a brown leather handbag. Further on was the body of a woman, almost fully clothed. She lay face downwards, her cheek resting on her left arm, her auburn hair against the dusty floor. Lewis noted that one shoe was still on her foot and that she wore no rings. Perhaps, if he had had time to reflect on the matter, he might have thought the absence of rings rather strange because Caroline Trayler was a married woman. Her husband of six months, a sergeant in the Durham Light Infantry, had been posted overseas two months earlier.

The officer in charge of the enquiry, Detective Inspector Francis Smeed of the Kent County Constabulary, informed Dr Keith Simpson, the Home Office pathologist, who arrived in Folkestone within hours to conduct the post-mortem. Simpson saw that the girl had been strangled by a grip of considerable force. The killer's fingernails had torn the skin of her neck. He had no doubt that there had been consensual sex for on the calves of her legs was dirt from the floor where she had lain.

The pathologist thought that she must have begun to resist. Perhaps she changed her mind about him, wanted him to stop. Had he become

The Great Escape

suddenly rougher, more demanding, hurting her? And now it was rape and resistance. There was a struggle. She had been choked from the front but then, possibly in an effort to control her, he had throttled her from behind.

Clues? Under the fingernails, torn and broken in her attempt to escape him, Simpson found one rust-brown wool fibre. On her thighs six dark hairs, which were not hers. These were sent off to the Metropolitan Police Laboratory for analysis.

Meanwhile Detective Inspector Smeed was trying to piece together what was known about Caroline Trayler. She came over as an attractive girl with a vivaciou; manner. For the past two months she had worked as an usherette at the Central Cinema. She was described as 'a bright and jolly girl, good at her work and popular with her colleagues.' But what exactly had Caroline Trayler been doing in the hours before her murder? She lived not far from where her body was found. She had been at home with her parents on the Sunday morning and at one o'clock in the afternoon had left for the cinema. At the end of the programme she had gone home for tea and had returned to the cinema for the evening shift. The cinema cashier remembered her leaving at nine o'clock. And she also recalled that Caroline had been wearing her wedding and engagement rings. When she was found, as PC Lewis had noted, she had no rings on her fingers.

Straight after work Caroline had gone to a pub, the Mechanics Arms, and had stayed there until ten o'clock. The landlord recalled that she had been talking to a soldier and he saw them leave together.

At least three witnesses saw her after this in the company of a soldier. About 10.15 pm they were walking along Bradstone Avenue towards Black Bull Road. At 10.30 pm they were in St John's Road and ten minutes later a witness saw them talking together outside the empty shop where her body was found. But none of the witnesses could describe the soldier. After all, in those days nobody took particular notice of soldiers on the streets. There were so many of them.

Now, let's not conceal the identity of the man who killed Caroline Trayler. At this stage the police had no idea who had murdered the attractive, auburn haired girl. And the members of the Royal Artillery unit to which he belonged were equally unaware that they had a killer in their midst. From now on, however, the reader will not labour under this disadvantage. The killer of Caroline Trayler was 25-year-old

CAUGHT BY SCIENCE

♦

Hairs Trapped Soldier Killer Who Had "A Way With Him"

"News of the World" Special

A STRAND of hair found on a soldier's clothes and a fibre of wool taken from the finger-nail of a dead girl built up a case which ended at the Old Bailey in a 25-year-old gunner being sentenced to death.

His wife sat outside the court while he was admitting his un-... ...and ... the also...

because of its apparent contradiction of everything known about the murderer.

• JEKYLL AND HYDE

In the Mechanics' Arms, Folkestone, where he "picked up" Caroline Trayler, he seemed a carefree, charming companion, glad of the friendship of a pretty girl. Within an hour of committing murder he was again the helpful soldier, anxious to assist a pretty W.A.A.F. officer by carrying her luggage along a lonely, dark road on his way back to

Finally Leckey was run to earth in London. Specimens of his hair were found by Dr. Simpson to correspond with those found on the girl. The orange fibres under her nails corresponded with those from his Army shirt.

Leckey admitted that he had ... with the ... within ...

Extract from the News of the World, *26 September 1943.*

Gunner Dennis Edmond Leckey from Manchester. His movements on the Sunday and over the next week are easily documented.

On the Sunday, a group of soldiers, including Leckey, had come by truck into Folkestone from their camp five miles outside the town. Leckey and his friend, Lance Bombardier Kenneth Knight, went to a cinema and then visited an amusement arcade. Later they visited several pubs, arriving at the Mechanics Arms at about nine o'clock. Knight was to say later that Leckey, described as tall, dark and handsome, was instantly attracted to the auburn haired girl who came in at about the same time. He got into conversation with her and bought her a drink. Poor Knight was more or less ignored as Leckey and the girl talked together for half an hour or so. So Knight took off, telling Leckey that he would see him on the truck back to camp, which was due to leave at 10.20 pm. And that was the last that Knight saw of Leckey until the following morning.

All the police had to go on was that they were looking for a soldier, a thankless task in wartime, with the military constantly on the move, going on manoeuvres, being posted to other units, being sent overseas, going on leave. There was a never-ending coming and going, which made it difficult for the police to follow up leads and suspects. Perhaps they hoped that in some way the murderer would contrive to give himself away. And that is precisely what Leckey eventually did.

It was 1.30 am when Leckey returned to camp. He told the guard commander, Sergeant Read, that he had been seeing a girl home. Although he had by now been absent without leave for nearly two hours, the sergeant seems not to have reported him. Perhaps he felt a serviceman might occasionally need to break the rules.

When Knight spoke to Leckey at breakfast time he thought his friend rather downcast but concluded it was a hangover. He was surprised that Leckey had not caught the second truck back to camp at 11.10pm. Had he spent the night with the girl, Knight asked. No, Leckey told him. He'd kissed her, that was all. She'd told him she had a date and they had parted. On the way back, he said, shortly after midnight, he had met a WAAF officer at Folkestone Junction station, and had carried her bag for her. This was later verified. But it might reasonably be asked what Leckey was doing in Folkestone at this time. This was never clarified but it does seem possible that he hung about in the empty shop until the streets had quietened down, though why he drew attention to himself with the WAAF officer remains a mystery.

In the course of the week Leckey was greatly preoccupied. He must have been constantly worrying about what he ought to do once the body was discovered. He was silent, forgetful, distracted, at times absenting himself from his work. He was reprimanded for not maintaining his vehicle properly. This was out of character as normally Leckey worked well. Now he was noticeably careless.

On the Thursday when the body was discovered Leckey made his decision to go absent without leave and began his preparations. He knew that to survive as a deserter he needed money and documentation. He stole a pad of leave forms, officially stamped, from the orderly room. If he were to be picked up by military policemen he could take a leave form out of his pocket and show it to them. All he had to do was fill in a new form so that the dates were correct and, of course, forge the signature of an officer.

Pay-books were perhaps less easy to come by for they were also a form of identity card and bore a photograph. But a resourceful man could get round that. Leckey stole four pay-books from members of his unit and therefore furnished himself with four more identities. All he needed to do was to take the photograph from one of the pay-books and insert his own. He knew this would enable him to talk his way into another camp, say that he was on detachment to a particular unit, tell the pay clerks that he had not been paid at his last posting, present one of the stolen pay-books and then, after payment, disappear, possibly after having a meal in the mess and even a bed for the night. That is perhaps how Leckey thought he might manage to keep out of the way of any Folkestone policemen who might turn up to question him. On the other hand, he knew that his desertion might raise suspicions where none had existed previously.

It was an old and tested ruse and Gunner Fred Latham, who slept in the next bed to Leckey, did not realise that his pay-book was missing until the Friday evening, just as he was getting ready to go out. It did not occur to him to suspect Leckey, who by this time had left the camp.

Ready money was also important to a man going on the run. Leckey had borrowed six shillings from Knight on the Friday, telling his friend that he had been lent money by another gunner, George Melia, earlier in the week and wanted to pay him back. Leckey and Melia appear to have been quite friendly. On the Friday morning Leckey told him that he was going home for the weekend. Melia advised him not to be so foolish because he was not entitled to leave just then. Couldn't he wait, Melia had asked? He would be due for leave in a week or two. No, Leckey had told him, he had to go. He said, quite unjustifiably, that he suspected his wife was being unfaithful to him. So the deserter who failed to turn up on guard duty at 7 pm was on the 8.40 pm train from Euston. And Melia, on official leave, and not wholly unsympathetic to a man whose wife was cheating, travelled with him from Euston to

Manchester. Melia also lost his pay-book that Friday, possibly during the train journey, but he in turn did not suspect that it had anything to do with his comrade.

Leckey's wife was surprised when her husband turned up. She was not expecting him for another week or so. He told her that he was on 48 hour embarkation leave. That accounted for his sudden arrival. But did Leckey now think it would all blow over? Did he think that he might be caught and serve time for desertion but that the murder of Caroline Trayler would be forgotten? Did he imagine that he would soon be able to join his wife and two children and settle down to a normal life? Or did he intend to disappear forever? Such thoughts must have bothered him. His mother-in-law, who spoke of her daughter's happy marriage, noticed that Leckey appeared to be worried. He told her, 'I've had a bit of bad luck the last three weeks.' He said that he had been to a birthday celebration, had drunk a bit too much and had seemed to lose his head a little. Then his pal, Ken, had gone off and left him. But Leckey never gave more than this broad outline of what it was that disturbed him so.

Quite how much his wife was privy to what had occurred in her husband's life is uncertain. He had told her he was on embarkation leave but what did she think when he departed from the house in Manchester for the last time on Sunday, 20th June? He left his uniform behind. Did his wife now suspect that her husband was on the run? And if she did, was she aware that it was because of a murder?

Now wearing civilian clothes but armed with pay-books and leave passes, Leckey sought out another artilleryman, John Kearney, in Stockport. Leckey told him he was returning to Folkestone and had to be back in camp by midnight the next day, Monday, 21st June. He asked if Kearney could find him a bed in his barracks for the night? It was easy enough. Here was a soldier, properly documented. He couldn't be refused. So Leckey spent the night in the drill hall at Mere.

The next day, before Leckey went for his train, the two men had a lunchtime drink. In the course of conversation Leckey mentioned that he had an engagement ring in his pocket. Someone had given it to him, he said. Was this one of Caroline Trayler's rings? Why did Leckey mention the ring? Did he hope that Kearney might buy it from him?

Despite what he had told Kearney, Leckey did not make for Folkestone. The next day, 22nd June, he was at Stafford railway station talking to a fellow-passenger, Mrs Winifred Woolley, who was travelling to Birmingham. He passed himself off as an RAF pilot officer, explaining to her why he was in civilian clothing. He preferred it to uniform, he said. He told her that he had lost his luggage and thought it was in Birmingham railway station. At New Street station he made enquiries at the left-luggage office and this must have convinced the lady of his sincerity. He stayed the night with her and the next day they went back to London where they parted.

For the next few days Leckey stayed at the Imperial Hotel, Russell Square but he was not afraid to go out and enjoy himself. He is heard of at the Queen's Hotel in Leicester Square in the company of Canadian and American non-commissioned officers. He spends an agreeable night at the Green Park Hotel. These few days seem to be an almost carefree interlude. But he was being looked for.

And it all came to an end. The great escape was over. On Tuesday, 29th June, Leckey was picked up at the City of Quebec public house. Constable Riggs told him that he resembled a man wanted for the theft of a wallet and contents and also for questioning by Folkestone police. 'You have got nothing on me,' Leckey told him. Asked his name, Leckey replied 'Latham'. He was taken to Marylebone police station to await the arrival of Detective Inspector Smeed from Folkestone.

Meanwhile the police went to Leckey's room at the Imperial Hotel. Here they found two pay-books, both in the name of Gunner Frederick Latham. Several pages had been extracted from one of the books and replaced by pages from Leckey's own pay-book. He had managed to draw 85 shillings in advance pay on this book. Also found were pay-books belonging to George Melia, and two other former army colleagues, Alan Hadley and Ronnie Fletcher. Other items included the pad of leave forms, Winifred Woolley's National Savings certificate book, her landlady's clothing coupons, a wallet containing £5 10 shillings, a watch and other papers belonging to two other servicemen. There were also hotel bills made out in the name of Alan Hadley.

The morning after his arrest Leckey was interviewed by Inspector Smeed, who told him that he was investigating the murder of Caroline Trayler. 'I know about it,' Leckey told him. Smeed asked him if he would make a statement. 'I was with the girl,' Leckey answered. 'I want to be fair with you and with myself and before I make a statement I should like to get advice.'

Dennis Leckey was tried before Mr Justice Singleton at the Old Bailey in September 1943. As far as the prosecution was concerned the case against him must have seemed watertight. There was the conduct of the accused from the time of the murder until his arrest. Was it not typical of a man with a guilty conscience, of a man trying to hide his identity? There was Knight's evidence that Leckey had talked to the girl in the Mechanics Arms on the night of the murder. There was the landlord's evidence that they had left the pub together. There were various inconsistent statements that Leckey made concerning the girl he had been seen with in the Mechanics Arms. And there was the scientific evidence.

Scientific evidence was called to show that the hairs which had been found on the murdered girl's thighs were identical to hairs of the accused; to show that the woollen rust-coloured fibre found under her fingernail came from the kind of khaki shirt which Leckey wore on the night of the murder; to show that on his trousers, which police had taken from his home in Manchester, was one auburn-coloured hair identical to Caroline Trayler's hair.

Whilst neither woollen fibre from a standard army issue shirt nor identical hairs offered absolutely compelling evidence – neither carried such detail as fingerprints – they did offer strong circumstantial evidence.

In view of the weight of argument against him, it was not surprising that after 30 minutes the jury returned a verdict of guilty. Leckey was sentenced to death.

At the perhaps inevitable appeal, Leckey's counsel claimed that there had been a misdirection of the jury at the trial. When Detective Inspector Smeed had first interviewed Leckey and told him that he was investigating the murder, Leckey had replied, 'I know about it.' Then he had said, 'I was with the girl. I want to be fair with you and with myself and before I make a statement I should like to get advice.' This, counsel pointed out, was not a denial of the charge but nor was it an admission. Leckey had said that he would say nothing until he had spoken to a solicitor. He was then recommended by the solicitor to say nothing that might incriminate him. In consequence Leckey did not appear in any witness box.

But in his summing up, Mr Justice Singleton, a highly experienced judge, had commented three times on this reluctance to make a statement to the police. The implication of the judge's remarks was that such silence was tantamount to an indication of guilt. 'Of course, he is not bound to say anything,' the judge observed, 'but what would you conclude?' At the appeal, Mr Casswell, representing Leckey, said that what the judge had said to the jury was the same as saying, 'If a man says "I reserve my defence", then you may rely on the evidence against him showing that he is the man responsible for the crime charged.'

The Crown accepted that Leckey's decision to remain silent when cautioned by the police should not be held against him. Nevertheless, the prosecution argued that even had the remarks not been made, in view of the overwhelming strength of the case against the accused man the jury could not have arrived at any other conclusion.

The appeal judges, however, agreed with the defence case that the jury had been misdirected. There were safeguards built into English law, they pointed out, and these protected people accused of crimes. One safeguard was the right of an accused person to remain silent until he had taken legal opinion. Nor need the accused give evidence at his own trial. It must not be inferred that silence was an admission of guilt. In the present case, the judges said, there was much evidence which would have justified a verdict of guilty but the court could not say for certain what verdict the jury would have come to had it been properly directed. The case against Leckey was dismissed.

Astonishingly then, Dennis Leckey walked free. Criminologist Brian Lane's conclusion that 'Society had, on this thankfully rare occasion, become victim of its own impeccably fair legal system' is very apt.

For Leckey, the brutal murderer of Caroline Trayler, it was another great escape.

BIBLIOGRAPHY

Aspin, John *Frances Kidder: The Last Woman to be Hanged in Public* (self-published 1990)

Browne, Douglas *Sir Bernard Spilsbury: His Life and Cases* (White Lion 1976)

Gaute, J.H.H. and Odell, Robin *The Murderers' Who's Who* (Pan Books 1980)

George, Michael and Martin *Coast of Conflict* (SB Publications 2004)

Humphreys, Sir Travers *A Book of Trials* (Heinemann 1953)

Igglesden, Charles *A Saunter through Kent* (Kentish Express 1908)

Lane, Brian *Murder Guide* (Robinson 1991)

Morton, James *A Calendar of Killing* (Warner 1997)

Simpson, Keith *Forty Years of Murder* (Harrap 1978)

Wilson, Colin *The Mammoth Book of True Crime* (Robinson 1990)

Vincent W.T. *The Records of the Woolwich District, Vol 2* (Virtue c1880)

Eltham and District Times
Folkestone Chronicle
Folkestone, Hythe and District Herald
Folkestone Observer
Kent Messenger
Kent and Sussex Courier
Kentish Express
Kentish Gazette
Maidstone and Kentish Journal
Maidstone Telegraph
The Star
The Times
Bygone Kent
Fingerprint Whorld
Illustrated London News
Illustrated Police News
Master Detective
Murder Most Foul
The Police History Society Journal